No BS
ROI

Social and Interactive Marketing for your Medical Aesthetic Practice

Jake Laban & Christopher Hall

TABLE OF CONTENTS

FOREWORD:

• •

Insist On Metrics

"Social Media is Bullshit"

This is the title of a book written in 2012 by fellow author B.J. Mendelson[1].

This enjoyable read about the social media marketing industry is geared toward agencies whose sole purpose is to help business owners successfully navigate the world of social media. It asserts that agencies should assist these businesses in accumulating more Likes, followers, shout outs, retweets and +1's. As you might imagine, most of these companies are very successful at achieving these goals. All anyone has to do is click a mouse and – poof! Success!

Many of these agencies' clients even describe the immediate rush they get when their Facebook pages are opened and they see the small army of followers they've amassed overnight. Suddenly, thousands have decided to connect virtually to their businesses. Who wouldn't be flattered? Thrilled at these results, the business owner then rushes to re-enter his or her credit card number, giving the agency more money in return for more followers, more Likes, more +1's and more feel-good rushes.

---

1   http://www.amazon.com/dp/1250002958

That's great, but there are a few problems with this strategy. The primary ones being:

- Banks do not accept Facebook Likes as deposits
- Creditors do not consider Twitter followers to be an appropriate form of payment
- Employee salaries cannot consist of Google Plus +1's

For all these reasons and more, you need to ensure that your business – and your social media efforts – actually makes money!

It seems that the entire social media marketing industry has been successful in deceiving the public that fundamental business-building strategies and metrics somehow do not apply to this new world of social media.

Why and how these vanity metrics have become the defining characteristics of business success make no logical sense until you realize the motivators behind it.

Unfortunately, Mendelson is correct. Our industry is full of bullshit. What's worse, the pile is getting bigger and bigger thanks to ego and vanity! If the goal of your business is to make money (and, in all likelihood, it is), then the results of your social media efforts must align with this goal or what's the point? For this reason alone, success on social media should never be measured by Likes, followers or +1's. Vanity metrics like these do not equate to business success.

Who We Are

Founded in 2011, Total Social Solutions LLC was created to provide business owners with an opportunity to create real and measurable business results through common-sense interactive marketing that includes social media.

Here at our Las Vegas headquarters, we don't have clients or customers.

We have partners, and, like any other company, we are not successful if our partners are not successful.

With that in mind, this book is dedicated to our partners. It has been an honor to work alongside these partners to develop new ways of approaching interactive marketing and social media as drivers of real business growth. Together we are revolutionizing the way success is measured on these innovative and relatively new platforms.

We show our partners measured business improvements through an increase in:

- Phone calls
- Service inquiries
- Revenue

What we are collectively achieving with our partners has caught the attention of groups throughout the Western Hemisphere. We are literally changing what it means to achieve true value in social media marketing.

Social media and interactive marketing can be new and scary concepts for many businesses. Companies often decide to try things out on interactive and social media simply out of the fear that they will fall behind if they don't. Regrettably, this fear-driven decision typically leads to even more panic once the business owner realizes that a dozen new networks have popped up since his interactive marketing plan was put in place! That kind of revelation is often motivation enough for the poor soul to throw his hands up in despair, frustration and intimidation. This doesn't sound like a fundamentally sound strategy that can lead to increased revenue, if you ask us. To us, it sounds like a reactive stance to business growth.

That's why we work with our partners on a more proactive stance that accepts interactive marketing for what it really is: a vehicle for creating a super-charged customer relationship infrastructure within a fast-paced, dynamic atmosphere. The strategies and tactics outlined in this book can be applied to any business-to-consumer (B2C) company that wants to have more intimate, engaging and profitable relationships with its customers.

Now, of course, we've learned a few things along the way. We'd kind of consider ourselves graduates (or at least attendees) of the School of Hard Knocks. While we don't display our diplomas on the wall, we've made sure to every lesson that school has imparted upon us. We've internalized, cried and improved - crafting a better service experience for our partners along the way.

Sure, maybe we shouldn't have told you that we cried that one time, but we believe transparency is an important part of any business relationship, and we pride ourselves on our honest commitment to you. That's why this book is written for you, the business leader, in the spirit of transparency. Throughout the following pages, we'll share lots of stories that we've picked up along our journey. We'll reveal the good, the bad and the ugly as we help you avoid the latter two on your own pathway to higher profits. Happy trails!

CHAPTER 1:

• •

Planning Your Success

Planning for success is a life strategy that reaches far outside the business world.

Basketball phenomenon Michael Jordan often spoke about visualization being one of the keys to his success on and off the court. He holds a string of athletic accolades, not the least of which includes his title as ESPN's Athlete of the 20th Century.

Swimmer Michael Phelps also utilizes this technique before he gets into the water. The 22-medal Olympian visualizes himself executing the perfect meet before he's even set foot in the pool.[2]

When athletes use visualization, they mentally prepare for every step of their competition. Done correctly, this technique is often surprisingly effective, allowing the athletes to execute their plans successfully.

The term visualization does a disservice to the process. By walking through every step of your success, you are forcing yourself to make decisions in advance. Often in the moment of crisis, it's difficult to maintain the perspective required to make a good decision. By making the tough choices before they're critical, you free yourself up to focus on other, time-critical

---

2   http://visualizingbirth.org/article-michael-phelps-says-visualization-his

issues. You'll make better surprise decisions, because your predictable decisions are already made. As you might expect, this technique is useful in business as well.

You've Got to Have a Plan

You can dramatically increase your chances of success in any endeavor through methodical, detailed planning. In the same way that a good surgeon makes sure that she has the necessary tools available before starting a surgery, a business owner can plan for success (or failure) in advance and increase the value of investments. This book is very deliberately designed as a tutorial. As you progress, please resist the temptation to leap ahead and begin mapping out your interactive and social media marketing plan. We believe it's best to learn about good marketing practices before planning your own success. An exercise will appear at the end of this book to guide you through your plan once you've learned everything there is to know about social media marketing (we promise!).

Know Your Business Drivers

Understanding what inputs affect the pace of your business is Step 1 of any marketing plan. If you're a pizza delivery company, it's pretty clear that more incoming phone calls will deliver more overall sales. If you're an internet retail store, then more people browsing your website will deliver more online sales. Select a few business drivers that you think you can affect, and focus your marketing efforts on those.

Select a Time Frame

Given the pace and cycle of your business, select a time frame that will allow you to patiently and consistently execute a strategy. Then be prepared to measure the results. Note that you must be keenly aware of your own business cycles to choose an appropriate time and time frame. It's important to select a realistic time frame that is long enough for you to execute your plan and monitor measurable business results.

Just as no two people are the same, no two businesses are alike. Your specific product mix, geography and client demographic will combine to make a unique business profile. The guidelines in this book are general, and you're going to have to experiment to find answers that work well for you. Treat every marketing plan as a sequence of experiments from which you can learn a little more about marketing solutions that work for you.

For any marketing plan, first select a time frame during which you can execute at least three different, related marketing experiments. For example, if you are typically measure quarterly results, then consider running three different but related marketing experiments. Compare and contrast your results at the end of the quarter.

This time frame becomes an important part of the iterative marketing process. Learning from these successes and failures is what helps us deliver better results over time.

Set Goals

Every marketing plan needs goals. You should have a strong grasp of your company's current performance, as well as a gauge of how much you can affect that performance with marketing, before you begin setting goals.

All goals should follow the SMART acronym[3]:

- **S**imple
- **M**easurable
- **A**ttainable

---

3   As originally referenced by George T Doran in "There's a S.M.A.R.T. way to write management's goals and objectives." November of 1981

- **R**elevant
- **T**imely

Develop a Plan

Time and time again, we come across small business owners who suffer from decision fatigue. Every month, they are asked to decide what their next steps are in terms of marketing and business operations. Unfortunately, with this mindset, many of these owners will eventually give up.

"It's too hard to keep up with things" and "I just got tired of running the same specials" are two of the most popular excuses we hear when a business owner explains why his plan failed. Many will cease their marketing efforts altogether and simply move onto other things after they've reached a certain level of frustration, boredom or lack of results.

By developing a plan, you avoid decision fatigue. Invest your time up front by developing your marketing strategy's blueprint. This way, you can spend the rest of the year executing this blueprint instead of remaining bogged down in the decision-making process and minute details. In essence, take a little time to make some good decisions once and benefit from them over time. Having a plan in place dramatically increases the likelihood that you'll be able to successfully execute your plan for the entire time frame. Think about it…once you've got your plan is place the hardest part of your work is already completed!

Predict Your Results

You should always, always have an expectation of results from a marketing activity. The very act of thinking through probable results will help you make better marketing decisions. You will gain a much better understanding of your client base if you're able to compare your actual results against your predicted results. With any luck, your predicted results should come very close to meeting the realistic goals you set.

Execute

Once again, all the planning and goal-setting in the world is useless if you don't see it through. Fortunately for you, with the hard work already done, it's easier than ever to simply put your plan in place and watch it play out.

Evaluate Your Results

Here's where your predictions meet reality (and hope they didn't wind up at different bars across town from each other!). By measuring these two indicators, you'll gain a valuable understanding of your clientele and how they make decisions. This insight will help you develop stronger, more targeted marketing campaigns in the future.

Measuring success is the most important part of this entire exercise. If you can't measure the results, you have no way to tell if your plan is working. Whether you're executing the plan yourself or working with a contractor or marketing agency, if the ultimate measurement of your results is "measurement is too hard," then you need to find someone else to handle your marketing.

Can you imagine starting a diet, toiling away at the gym and then realizing there's no way to measure results? No scales, no mirrors, no public feedback, no loose-fitting pants to help you gauge how much weight you've lost? If you invest your time and energy in something, and realize there is no way to track your progress, you're going to give up pretty quickly. You know what they say about trees that fall in uninhabited woods…

We'll talk about measuring success in detail later in the book. In the meantime, rest assured that technology allows you to automatically measure and report on foot traffic, incoming phone calls, website clicks, coupon redemptions, and much more. Measurement of your results has never been easier, and you benefit as a result.

Aim for Improvement

Evaluating your results is absolutely the most important part of any approach. Your situation will always be unique because your business, clientele, geographic location, etc. will always be unique to you and your target audience. Once you've taken a look at what you've done, however, it is critical for you to figure out if and how you can alter your methods to achieve even better results. Remember, there is *always* room for improvement. Just ask Michael Jordan or Michael Phelps!

So these are your planning steps. You can thank us for revealing them in Chapter 1 by refraining from slamming this book shut and running out to conquer the world so early in your social media marketing game. Trust us, we've got a lot more to say about marketing platforms and best practices. And this is definitely not the last you'll see of these steps. We'll be revisiting them again – as well as providing you with a handy planning template – later on in this book.

CHAPTER 2:

. . . .

Business Growth Basics

"How Do I Grow My Business?!"

This is the single biggest question any business owner will face. Obviously, there are lots of ways to grow a business. In fact, there is an endless list of ideas that business owners have successfully employed over the years. Though ideas may be endless, the fundamental strategies behind them remain relatively unchanged.

When laying the groundwork for additional business-building discussions, realize that virtually *all* business-building ideas fit into one of three categories:

1. Recruitment
2. Conversion
3. Retention

You must understand each of these strategies – as well as their implications on your budget – before you can even begin to brainstorm.

A Background in Business Growth

The traditional marketing paradigm used to be one in which your brand sent out a message to your target audience. It was a one-way communication channel. This paradigm was limited by the communication channels of the times, which were entirely one-directional. Nowadays, with interactive and social media, there exists a two-way communication channel. You know who is receiving your message and they, in turn, have an opportunity to message you back.

This requires a shift in the way you think about marketing. It used to be all about getting your message out as loudly, proudly and frequently as you could. Through platforms like television, radio, billboards, *Yellow Pages* and others, mass media promotions were all one-way channels. You simply broadcasted your message to your audience, with no opportunity for them to reply. Now that today's two-way channels exist, your brand must motivate people to follow you on interactive marketing platforms.

That's what you're doing in social media. You're connecting. You're building a community.

Print is Dead

The proof is out there. The print media graveyard is riddled with all sorts of iconic brands. The *Saturday Evening Post*, *Life* and *Newsweek* magazines were all iconic periodicals. And now they're out of print. Even Oprah had a magazine that went belly-up! The reason for their demise is easy to spot. It's because advertisers are not directing their money at print advertising anymore. Instead, it has all gone online. By 2011, the amount of money spent on digital advertising in the U.S. had outpaced what was spent on print advertising. Many reputable industry sources believe this trend will never reverse.

It's definitely true that consumers are turning to digital media more frequently. This is particularly true in the U.S. Think about your current journal, magazine and newspaper subscriptions compared to just 1 year ago. Chances are, the amount of print publications you receive has dropped significantly.

The Usefulness of Social Media

From the perspective of a business owner, the information social media and interactive channels can offer you regarding your potential customers is invaluable. Social media networks provide detailed demographic and personality data about your audience that was never accessible before. This is especially true when compared to the limited information print advertisers had available to them. In traditional marketing programs, you had no idea who was actually *seeing* your advertisement. Today, the data that can be mined through interactive and social media is incredibly powerful.

Let's not forget one thing. Your target audience has a lot of power, too! A 1978 study for Coca Cola tells that a satisfied customer tells an average of 1 person about his or her experience with a business, while an unsatisfied customer would tell 10[4]. That is multiplied today due to the interactive and social media channels. Any one of your customers can broadcast their every rant or rave to their respective networks…and some of your customers have thousands of connections! Social media and interactive marketing provide your business – and your consumers – with a *massive* force multiplier that can be applied to your recruitment, conversion and retention efforts.

---

4   From the TARP study, referenced here http://www.tarp.com/news_tarp_milestones.html

Recruit...New Customers

Simply put, recruitment is the act of getting potential customers to make their first purchases. In its most popular form, this is simply known as advertising. The impact of recruitment efforts on a business' advertising budget is significant. Large corporate entities have significant cash they can use to pull large outbound advertising initiatives that target potential buyers across multimedia platforms.

Because of this, small business owners often feel like they're behind the 8-ball with respect to advertising. They've been taught that they need to advertise and that, if they don't advertise, they will fall behind the competition.

Recruiting new customers to your business requires the greatest amount of financial investment for a small business owner because due to the high level of ad spend waste that is inherent in mass advertising. For example, a magazine ad targeting women in their 40s will likely be seen by many people who do not fit this demographic. Interactive marketing technologies, on the other hand, have revolutionized the ways in which marketers can reach their target groups.

4. Convert...the Same Customers with New Products

Converting customers from one product line to another can be one of the more financially rewarding and efficient ways to grow your business. Many business books have stated that customer acquisition costs are one of the highest costs a business will face. Once the business owner has a customer, converting this customer into purchasing multiple product lines allows the business owner to maximize the lifetime value of the customer relationship.

Conversion strategies are often known as upsell or cross-selling tactics, strategies in which the consumer receives a notification that a new product or service is available. These notifications can be made when they're purchasing another product, such as through a direct mailing piece or, in the case of interactive marketing, in the form of an email or Facebook post sent to the community of customers.

With these tools in place, it becomes obvious just how important it is to have a robust customer relationship management (CRM) system. While this may sound daunting and expensive, a CRM system can be as simple as storing all your electronic customer contact information in one centralized location. CRM can refer to any system that allows you to quickly pull contact list reports by product type purchased for the purpose of sending out email notifications.

Getting your current customers to purchase other products has major positive budget implications. This is not only because of the additional revenue that's being delivered, but also because it inherently implies that this customer will not be purchasing that product from a competing entity. A successful conversion to a second (or even third) product line adds another opportunity for a positive touch point with your business, and a higher chance of long-term customer retention.

5. Retain...the Same Customers, for Repeat Purchases

As you can see below, business books differ on the costs-savings analysis outlined below. While the specific numbers range, one thing is clear... getting new customers is expensive! Specifically:

- It's five to seven times less expensive to keep an old customer than to acquire a new one!
- Acquiring a new customer through advertising is 12 to 20 times more expensive than keeping a customer happy who keeps coming back!
- It costs 10 to 15 times as much to establish a new customer relationship versus taking care of your good customers!

Whichever source you listen to, one thing is clear: the numbers are all over the place. The specific costs differentials tend to vary industry to industry. However, at the end of the day, all that matters is your understanding that the least expensive way to preserve future sales and cash flow is to keep your customers happy. By keeping them happy, you keep them coming back.

This is an important point as it understates one key business maxim, and that is "a dollar is a dollar." Whether this dollar comes from a new customer or existing customer does not matter to you. Your business invests time, money and resources to get people coming in the door…make sure they don't just walk out the back!

Many business owners hear this message, get excited and immediately start thinking about how they'll reach out to these customers to get them back inside their business. Unfortunately, this logic is flawed. It skips over an incredibly important step…ensuring that the customer experience is as good as it can possibly be!

Once a system is in place that can deliver consistently positive customer experiences, you will easily see how an effective set of retention systems can mean the difference between your business being simply successful and your business being hugely successful! Happy, repeat customers allow the business owner to easily and inexpensively increase the lifetime value of the customer relationship, thereby driving profitability for the long term.

CHAPTER 3:

∙∙

The Basic Tools Of Marketing

Crafting Promotions

The American Marketing Association defined marketing in 2007 as:

> *Marketing is the activity, set of institutions, and processes for creating, communicating, delivering and exchanging offerings that have value for customers, clients, partners and society at large.*[5]

Business schools across the world teach the four Ps of marketing:

1. Product
2. Price
3. Promotion
4. Place

Marketing is a huge topic! As much as we might try, this book may never replace an $80,000 Ivy League MBA. Instead, we will focus largely on the third "P," promotion, to drive value for your business. We're specifically going to drill down some basic principles that can help you create effective

---

5   http://www.marketingpower.com/aboutama/pages/definitionofmarketing.aspx

messaging that emphasizes the existence, quality, and value of your product, brand or service.

Delivering crisp, effective messaging is even more important in today's abbreviated messaging environment. There's no doubt that communications are getting shorter and shorter. Consumers today are bombarded with messages from everyone, including their friends, family, favorite celebrities, advertisers and colleagues. It's tough to stand out in this noisy environment; so you must learn to craft a reliable, concise, interesting promotional message. To put it another way, get to the point!

People have been studying what can make or break a certain strategy or technique for thousands of years. Do you think cavemen created fire the very first time two sticks came into contact with one another? We think not. While many of today's effective fire-starting techniques have already been fleshed out, there are plenty of ways you can analyze *your* business strategies as you develop your marketing plan.

Know Your Audience

You probably already know what your target customer looks like. He or she fits into a certain income bracket, age range and level of education. Your target demographic probably favors one gender over the other. If you can accurately pinpoint your target customer, then you know that this particular type of person is more likely to spend money with you than the general population is. You probably know the likes, dislikes, and even a few items or catch phrases that will capture the attention of this particular client profile.

This information is critical when it comes to designing effective promotions. How critical, you ask? We ran our own suite of experiments to show you exactly how the proper messaging can affect your ability to cause action. Net results-wise, we were able to create *more than four times as many customer actions* by simply taking the time to properly word our messaging

Learn Through Experimentation

In order to figure out what sort of messaging works, we turned to the world's biggest laboratory: the internet (specifically, search-based advertising).

Google has created an online marketplace that allows businesses to connect with anonymized consumers on a mind-boggling scale. Given an advertising budget, you can share your message with millions of people, and collect data about their reactions to that message.

Comparing the results from different advertising messages on Google provides valuable insights about how an anonymous audience reacts to those messages. From this, we can infer rules about how effective messaging can be to that audience.

For our experiment, we chose a U.S.-wide test audience of women ages 25 to 40.

We created an imaginary product, car tires. We chose this product for several reasons, including:

- Tires are a largely commoditized product. There is often very little perceived difference between tires, which makes marketing messages quite striking
- Online advertising for tires is inexpensive, therefore we were able to run more experiments within our budget
- Most of our target demographic can be assumed to own a car, and are therefore likely to be consumers of our imaginary product

We ran many, many experiments around messaging. In the end, we were able to craft a single final iteration that displays the major characteristics that confirm our theories about messaging. A summary may be found in the table below:

Ad-iteration	Hook	Message	Characteristics	Action rate
1	95,000 mile tire warranty	Soft rubber, durable and an incredible warranty!	Feature-based messaging	Baseline
2	Don't buy tires for seven years	Safe, quiet tires last practically forever!	Benefit-based messaging	2x baseline
3	Don't buy tires for seven years	Safe, quiet tires last practically forever. Click here now!	Benefit-based messaging Call to action Urgency	4x baseline 2x ad #2
4	Don't buy tires for seven years	Hurry, and get safe, quiet tires that last practically forever. Click here now!	Benefit-based messaging Call to action Urgency highlighted	4.3x baseline 2.2x Ad #2 1.1x Ad #3

We'll talk about the characteristics of the ads in this chapter. As you can see, proper messaging increased the action rate *4.3 times* over the baseline of our experiment.

The lesson here is that if you can deliver marketing basics in every message, you can expect to see dramatically improved results. Your phone should ring more, people should walk into your store more frequently and, when they do, you will sell more items.

Understand the Differences Between Features and Benefits

There is a wealth of information about the differences between selling a feature and selling a benefit. It's not enough just to understand your audience. You must understand why they will purchase your product, as well.

The differences between features and benefits can be subtle. Let's take, for example, a breast augmentation procedure. Here are some real examples from surgical product and surgeons' websites:

Feature	Benefit
Up to 450 CC implants	Get the size you want
I-Flow pain relief system	Quick, minimal-pain recovery
Sub-pectoral plane augmentation placement	Look natural
TUBA breast augmentation	No scarring, leave people wondering if it's natural or not

Look at the first row. Many patients may not know what size implants they want or need. Patient education is important, but during the sales process, it's important to give patients the information that they want ("we can deliver the size you want") rather than technical jargon they may not understand.

Your target audience may be able to instantly understand a benefit from reading about a feature, or they might need your help. Understanding how they think about your product or service is critical to successfully differentiating your messaging.

Benefit/feature messaging is not always a black-and-white discussion. With practice, you'll be able to deliver effective, benefit-based messaging in no time.

The results of this are powerful. Through our in-house experiments, we have found that benefit-based messaging was twice as likely to motivate an audience into action as feature-based messaging. This simple change in your messaging can double the effectiveness of your promotional campaigns.

To get a better sense of what we're talking about, it's helpful to look at your promotions from the audience's perspective. Ask yourself what your client would ask. This tends to boil down to *what's in it for me?* From that perspective, the answer often becomes obvious.

> **Fun Fact**
>
> Testimonials are just another "What's In It For Me" message. When you view a testimonial, what the marketer is telling you is, "You can be just like this person." Use this when crafting your own testimonials, and make them feel more like they're coming from your intended audience.

Call to Action

Unfortunately, many marketers fall into an easy trap when working on new media platforms like social media and email marketing. They fail to explain *how* a potential customer can take advantage of a promotion. Demand creation is futile if we don't make it clear how our customers can act on our offers.

Today's short messaging platforms make this even more important. It's not always easy for us to fit the right content into the limited space we're given, so developing a concise call-to-action can deliver a big change in your results.

Can you see the difference?

Message 1: *You can save $50 off your next hair style appointment!*

Message 2: *You can save $50 off your next hair style appointment! Call (888) 626-3660 now and book a visit today!*

Message 1 is compelling. Your hair is getting unmanageable anyway, why not save $50 off your next appointment? The challenge is that you aren't being told exactly how to act on this incredible offer. Because life is distracting, you may not get around to scheduling your appointment because you have to look up the proper phone number and make that call.

Message 2 adds a single line that explains how you can make this offer a reality. Furthermore, it uses the imperative (command) form of the action verb (call) to tell the reader how to act on this offer.

As we showed you earlier in Ad #3 above, this difference is striking. A simple appended phrase like "Click here" can double the customer action rate. That's right – it's that simple. Just tell people what they need to do and you could potentially *double* your response rate!

This book is a how-to, so we've put together a few easy phrases you can experiment with:

- Book Now
- Reserve Today
- Buy Now and Save
- Learn More Here
- Order Today
- Click Here
- Get a Free Estimate
- Join Us
- Upgrade Your Services

Urgency

Creating a sense of scarcity and urgency drives action. Think about it. What purchases have you made in the past year because you were worried a company was running out of stock, or that the item you desired might not be available later? This is the essence of an urgency purchase.

Here are some words and phrases that can impart a sense of urgency when integrated into your marketing strategies:

- Now
- Hurry
- Today
- While Supplies Last
- Memorial Day Special
- Only X Spots Left
- Don't Wait
- Before Time Runs Out
- Expires Today

By using language like this, you will raise the action rate on all your promotions. During our experiments, we noticed that something as simple as tacking the word "hurry" onto an advertisement could raise the action rate by as much as 10 percent (in Ad #4 above). It's an easy addition to make, and the results are well worth it.

Measure Your Results

You must select your key performance indicators (KPIs) for every marketing campaign. These KPIs will essentially become the goals of your campaign.

Take a long, hard look at how your business operates before you select your KPIs. Make sure each KPI you select can be a direct result of your marketing campaign, and not subject to the success/failure of other factors such as weather or your employees' abilities to close a sale.

Say you run a hair salon that is trying to attract more business. The hair salon gets new business in one of three ways:

1. Incoming Phone Calls
2. Walk-in Traffic
3. Online Appointment Requests

The goal of your advertising campaign is to drive more walk-in traffic. In order to do so, you are going to rent billboard space near the salon. By doing this, you hope the billboard will raise the salon's visibility, thereby creating more business.

Many business owners start out using overall business revenue as their KPI. It just makes sense. As a business owner, your ultimate goal is to drive up that overall revenue. At first blush, revenue appears to be a good KPI. The challenge becomes one of attribution. A rise in overall revenue could be the result of any number of factors, ranging from a competitor going out of business to a precisely executed marketing campaign. Your KPI must be one for which you can draw clear attribution to your marketing experiments. For these reasons and more, overall business revenue may be too broad of a business health indicator to accurately measure the effectiveness of your advertisements.

With revenue out, let's choose something more directly measurable. We're going to start by thinking of the three ways your hair salon gets new business. Some critical thinking leads us to the conclusion that a billboard will have a trivial effect on online appointment requests. It is reasonable to assume, however, that a billboard *can* drive walk-in traffic and even mobile phone calls.

Next, we'll decide how to measure this performance. An easy solution for walk-in traffic is to simply ask the client. Every time a client is greeted, she should be asked how she heard about the business. A simple tally sheet can capture the results, which can be used later on to measure the effectiveness of specific promotional campaigns. The framing of this question is important. The question "Did you see our billboard?" will likely yield a number of positive answers, while "Why did you decide to come see us?" will likely deliver a better idea of how attribution will work.

There are a few solutions to measure incoming phone calls. They can be tracked and recorded, and incoming callers can also be asked how they heard about the salon. Again, results can be measured periodically.

After a baseline performance has been established, you can launch your promotional campaign. Over time, you'll collect metrics that show the effectiveness of your billboard campaign as a business driver against your KPIs.

CHAPTER 4:

••

What Is Social Media And
Interactive Marketing?

Definition

The McGraw Hill dictionary defines interactive marketing as…

> *"Two-way buyer–seller electronic communication in a computer-mediated environment in which the buyer controls the kind and amount of information received from the seller."*

This same source defines social media as…

> *"The means of interactions among people in which they create, share, and exchange information and ideas in virtual communities and networks."*

Background and History

Let's take a bigger-picture look at what interactive and social media marketing really mean. As we discussed earlier, marketing allows you to establish your brand's identity, differentiate yourself as a community contributor and build awareness about your offerings.

In the 18th and 19th centuries, small business marketing was limited to the size of the sign (aka shingle) that hung outside your door. Alternatively, the small business owner could undertake other localized marketing efforts, such as hiring town criers or paying someone to hand out flyers.

In the early 20th century, and with the advent of new technologies like the high-speed printing press and fast-moving automobile, new advertising opportunities presented themselves in the form of roadside billboards, the *Yellow Pages* directory and national magazine advertisements.

After World War II, televisions and radios found their ways into every household. This brought about the true birth of what we now know as mass communications. With powerful tools like television and radio networks, businesses could get their messages out to millions of people by advertising on programs like CBS's *I Love Lucy* or Paul Harvey's radio newscast.

A digital revolution was born in the **mid-'90s** with the early mainstream expansion of the World Wide Web. Suddenly, American homes had access to the internet thanks to graphically intuitive browsers like Netscape and Microsoft Internet Explorer. By the **late '90s**, internet service providers (ISPs) like America Online (AOL) began to revolutionize the way Americans interacted with brands. Businesses learned to adapt, and started experimenting with internet advertising.

For the most part, all marketing activities up to this point were one-way. Regardless of whether the message was featured on a flyer, billboard, television, or as an internet banner, marketing was effectively a one-way flow of communication from the brand out to the targeted consumer.

Things began to shift dramatically during the turn of the millennium, however, during a period we call the digital revolution. This revolution continues to this day as we move through a time of massive, rapid changes in digital and interactive marketing.

In the Year 2000...

Let's look back at some of the marketing opportunities available in 2000. If your business wanted a website, you'd have to pay a good deal of money to have this built by a specialized digital agency. We'll call this a 'big website', due to the big expense! Even with professionals, it was very difficult and expensive to incorporate images and/or videos into your website. During that time, some early adopters paid for advertisements through Yahoo!, AOL and other online portals like AskJeeves. Millennial consumers were primarily computing through desktop computers, though they shifted to more portable laptop computers as the decade progressed.

Then in 2007...

Things really changed in 2007 when Steve Jobs and his Apple team introduced the iPhone®. Jobs described the iPhone® as a portable device that delivered "your life in your pocket," and it has delivered on that promise.

The iPhone®, and smartphones in general, are the ultimate digital devices. They have truly changed the face of small business marketing forever.

Never before has there been a device that allows us to broadcast our every thought, feeling, tweet, post, review and photo from wherever we are, at any time. Smartphones have revolutionized the way we interact with each other and the world around us. As a result, the internet was forced to become more mobile-friendly.

Today, the masses – which were once relegated to the role of simple recipient of information – can (and do) become publishers themselves.

Democratizing Publishing: Leveling the Playing Field

Thanks to smartphones, anyone can publish comments about a business and potentially reach *millions* of people immediately. The power that the average consumer now has was once reserved for media empire tycoons like William Randolph Hearst and Rupert Murdoch.

Your customers now have the power to leverage interactive marketing and social media for *your* business!

Social media, the central driver of all this, really caught fire in the mid-'00s. This platform is exactly where brands need to be if they want to thrive in today's economy. The fact is, people are talking about your brand, even if they aren't referring to you by name or on one of your digital spaces. This has become the new reality because people love to talk about their experiences, and they've found a great voice online.

Business owners need to lead brands that lead the discussions in their given industries. These are the companies that will be best positioned for success in the long run.

There is no debating that interactive and social media are changing the world we live in. The examples are all around us. They're in the 2008 presidential election, the Arab Spring uprising of early 2012 and the Occupy Wall Street (as well as its spin-offs) movement of that same year. Governments are being shaped and dictators are being overthrown with the exact same tools that small business owners have in their hands.

You, as a small business owner, have the opportunity to do amazing things with interactive and social media marketing.

Interactive Marketing IS Relationship Marketing

True, comprehensive interactive marketing is about much more than just social media. What is central to this discussion is the idea of growth through word of mouth or, what we call word of mouth marketing (WOMM).

Word of Mouth Marketing

Since the beginning of time, word of mouth marketing has been the most powerful form of advertising. When searching for a new good or service, the first place a person is likely to turn for advice is their own peer group. Friends don't tend to be secretive about the things they love…or the things they hate. Not only is word of mouth marketing the most powerful way for a brand to obtain credentialed referrals that will be well received by the new prospective customer (friend), but it also tends to be the least expensive form of advertising.

Interactive and Social Media Marketing IS Word of Mouth Marketing, En Masse

Consumers expect to engage with brands they love through interactive and social media. These platforms help brand marketers and business owners develop a sense of community…and this community is likely to buy more, and more often.

With this upside comes some downside, we're afraid. As the old saying goes "live by the sword, die by the sword." The power of instant communication means that a scathing review can be seen just as quickly and by just as many people as a positive review. This can sometimes amount to millions upon millions of people. Never before has your brand's reputation been exposed to more risk than it is right now.

If people like you and what you're selling, they're going to tell their friends. If they don't like you, what you're selling, your customer service or their overall experience, they're also going to tell their friends. Smartphones allow everyone to be a critic or a pundit. A ranter or a raver. While you may never win over 100 percent of the population, you can have a large effect on how your business is perceived.

Central to effective management of this is dialogue is a commitment to great customer service. There are volumes of wonderful books on this topic, so we will leave the customer service tips to the professionals. We'll simply say that interactive and social media places a huge magnifying glass on your business. It is also important to remember that whatever is written on the internet is written in stone, sort to speak, as it is not easily removed by anyone besides the person who wrote it.

For every wonderful and glowing review that our businesses get online, it is equally possible for us to receive a very negative review that needs to be balanced off and managed effectively.

Negative reviews about you and your business stink. They hurt. And the fact is, if you haven't received one yet, you need to do two things:

1. Consider yourself lucky
2. Prepare yourself, because you *will* someday incur a negative review

If your business has the proper systems and strategies in place, you will not only be able to effectively manage the inevitable negativity that everyone receives, but you'll be able to ride the wave of positive energy that your business also receives. It's through this wave that you can encourage your customers to become evangelists for you!

This is why it's absolutely critical to craft and execute a solid interactive and social media marketing strategy for the sake of your brand's health in this new digital world. When executed correctly, a solid interactive and social media marketing strategy can drive the type of advocacy your business needs.

Interactive Marketing

Interactive marketing is very new. It was ushered in with the advent of high-speed broadband internet and the omnipresence of smartphones. With all this technology and speed at our fingertips, you'll need to understand *what* tools exist for small business owners and *whom* they will want to target.

Fun Fact

Did you know that the average smartphone has more than 1,000 times the computing power of the spacecraft that safely carried man to the moon and back?

We'll specifically look at:

1. Email marketing
2. Social media marketing
3. Key influencers in interactive marketing

Email Marketing

Though it's now middle-aged, emails are more important and accessible than ever thanks to smartphones and tablet computers.

If a person wanted to check his or her CompuServe.com email inbox in the 1990s, they'd have to be tethered to a desk, awaiting a dial-up modem connection that would take several minutes to log them on. And you could just forget it if your email contained photos or graphics of any kind. You might as well go make yourself a sandwich and hope like heck no one called your land line, because you'd be in for a bumpy ride. Nowadays, we complain if our Wi-Fi takes longer than a second to download content!

Unfortunately, brand marketers had already learned how to use email to market their products and services. Spam email was a major issue by the time AOL made its debut in 1991. It took some time, but strict regulations were eventually put into place by Pres. George W. Bush's administration. Thanks to the CAN-SPAM Act of 2003, spammers are now aggressively pursued by the Federal Trade Commission and face both civil and criminal penalties.

Email marketing may have a long and storied past, but its power has never been greater thanks to the immediacy of technology. Just 10 years ago, the world lacked 4G and LTE wireless connectivity, making email a less powerful medium. In order for you to successfully get your business' message across, each individual you targeted had to be sitting in front of a desktop computer at home or at work. Or possibly at the library or a nearby internet café, but what were the chances of reaching someone there?

Now, small business owners can send an email to their audience, delivering messages straight to their smartphones, with a powerful call to action to motivate the purchase process.

The great news today is that every digital movement can be tracked. You, the small business owner, now have access to track actions driven as a result of your email campaigns.

These track actions include:

- Open rates
- When (time and date) the email was opened
- Who (names) opened the email
- Phone calls driven by the email
- Click-throughs and purchases driven by the email

Email marketing produces immediate, real-time results. Some of our clients have received phone calls within *five minutes* of sending an email! If that's not a measure of success, we don't know what is.

Social Media Marketing

Social media marketing is the use of social networking sites like Facebook, Twitter, Google+ and YouTube to promote commercial enterprises. Although these social sites were originally created for personal use, they are now effectively utilized by organizations of all sizes to communicate with current and prospective clients and partners. Social marketing is far different than the traditional marketing that most businesses continue to use today, specifically, TV, radio and print.

People tune in to traditional media for content they want to see. When an ad appears it is an interruption to that content stream. So what do they do? They fast forward, change the channel or simply avoid looking at it!

People are also spending more time watching videos online. It's not just YouTube, Hulu, Netflix and a number of other streaming providers. Large networks have even changed their models to adapt to this new shift in viewing habits. Owned by Google, the online video service YouTube is a massive disruptive force of change whose potential is just starting to manifest itself.

We'll put it to you this way: if your company wanted to get a nice video out there in the 1990s, you'd spend thousands – or even tens of thousands – having a production and editing crew come in to produce it. You'd then pay thousands more for the privilege of airing this video on a TV channel owned by one of the major corporations.

Now, with YouTube and other video-steaming social media platforms, your business can produce a video in-house. You can then create your *own channel*, which is branded with your name, logo, etc. The best part is that you can post as much as you want!

Many people associate social media with Facebook and Twitter. While that's fine, they should also know that social media was around long before the boom of 2010. Social media marketing actually has a very rich history, as outlined below:

A History of Social Networks[6]

1997	The first recognizable social network site launches. SixDegrees.com allowed users to create profiles and list their friends.
1998	Profiles existed on most major dating sites and many community sites although those friends were not visible to others.
1997-2001	A number of community tools began supporting various combinations of profiles and publicly articulated friends and cultural groups. Many of these tools are fashioned after instant messenger Buddy Lists. Classmates.com launches.
2000	SixDegrees closes. While people were already flocking to the internet, most did not have extended networks of friends who were online. Early adopters complained that there was little to do after accepting friend requests, and most users were not interested in meeting strangers. The service may have been ahead of its time.
2001	Ryze.com launches to help people leverage their business networks. Users were primarily members of the San Francisco business and technology communities. This included the entrepreneurs and investors behind many future social networking sites (SNSs) like Tribe.net, LinkedIn and Friendster.

---

6   Summarized from: Boyd, d. m. and Ellison, N. B. (2007), Social Network Sites: Definition, History, and Scholarship. Journal of Computer-Mediated Communication, 13: 210–230. doi: 10.1111/j.1083-6101.2007.00393.x

2002	Friendster launches as a social complement to Ryze. It was designed to help friends meet friends of friends, based upon the assumption that friends of friends would make better romantic partners than strangers would.
2003	Friendster's popularity surges. However, the site encountered technical and social difficulties. Servers and databases were ill-equipped to handle its rapid growth. The site faltered regularly, frustrating users.
2003-on	Many new SNSs launch. Most took the form of profile-centric sites that were trying to replicate the early success of Friendster or target specific demographics. Examples include professional sites like LinkedIn, Visible Path and Xing (formerly openBC), which focused on business people. There were also passion-centric SNSs like Dogste, activist sites like Care2, MyChurch for Christian churches and their members, Flikr for photo sharers and even Couchsurfing, which connected travelers to people with room on their couches.
August '03	Myspace launches in Santa Monica to compete with sites like Friendster, Xanga and AsianAvenue. It aims to attract estranged Friendster users after rumors emerged that Friendster would adopt a fee-based system.
January '04	Orkut.com is launched by Google but fails to build a sustainable U.S. user base. It was popular in Brazil throughout the decade, however.
2004	Teenagers begin joining MySpace en masse. Unlike older users, most teens were never on Friendster. Some joined simply because they wanted to connect with their favorite bands.
February '04	TheFacebook.com launched in Cambridge, Mass., as an exclusive service for anyone with an "@harvard.edu" email address.
February '05	YouTube is founded.

June '05	News Corporation purchases MySpace for $580 million, attracting massive attention to social media.
September '05	Facebook quietly grows by expanding to include high school students, professionals inside corporate networks and, eventually, everyone.
March '06	Twitter launches.
October '06	YouTube is purchased by Google for $1.6 billion.
November '07	Facebook launches Pages, forever changing the way small businesses present themselves in the social media world.
January '08	Facebook and ABC News co-sponsor the presidential debate.
November '08	Barack Obama wins the election, due in large part to effective leveraging of social media to re-engage with youth.
February '09	Facebook creates the Like button, bringing new meaning to the term.
2009	According to Brandwatch.com, nearly 2 billion tweets are sent on Twitter every quarter.
January 2010	The first off-earth tweet is sent by astronaut T.J. Creamer from the International Space Station.

Hopefully this vast history gave you a sense of just how crucial social media is and will be in the future. If you want to ensure your business' growth, you *must* start taking a closer look at social media marketing and the role it will play in the future health of your business.

What Does Success Look Like on Social Media?

One common misconception is that social media is all about attracting new customers. This fallacy often leads to significant disappointment once business owners realize they're not seeing the results in terms of new client acquisitions or an increase in sales. This is because this strategy does not focus on the people who are most likely to interact with their businesses through social media.

Success on social media means:

- Selling current and past customers new products and services (conversion)
- Selling current and past customers products and services more frequently (retention)
- Making it easy for your customers to spread the word about your business (referrals)

To be successful at social media marketing, it's important to remember that the consumer of social media is simply catching up with his or her friends and family. Advertisements from brands (even yours) are viewed as interruptions to this experience and can quickly become a nuisance. There is, however, a way to catch the consumer's eye while refraining from diminishing his or her social media experience. It's called balance. By contributing a healthy amount of non-promotional content to your social media community, you can actually *boost* the effectiveness of your promotional efforts.

In essence, you must learn to appreciate how pitching *less* will actually help you sell *more*!

This concept relates back to why people started using social media in the first place (connecting with friends and loved ones). They are not out shopping, and they are not looking to receive advertising messages. Therefore, to be successful you need to blend into this network of friends and family on social media. By becoming a friend, you can effectively penetrate some of the influential peer groups that can help drive your sales.

Key Influencers on Interactive Marketing

While there are certainly social media VIPs that your business will want to target, there are also some powerful peer groups of social media users that can supercharge your brand's growth.

Examples of influential peer groups on social media:

- Elite Yelpers
  Yelp is a powerful, review-based social network that promotes its most active Yelp users to Elite Yelper status. These people hold tremendous power as the reviews they write are far less likely to be filtered out by Yelp's powerful (and controversial) filter. You can benefit from this group by identifying Elite Yelpers who frequent your establishment. Yelp displays the names of local Elite Yelpers at http://www.yelp.com/elite#. The site is making these names and profiles public so you can reach out to them! You can even partner with Yelp on one of its Elite Yelper events, thereby putting you in direct contact with some of the most influential people the site has identified.

- YouTubers with Lots of Subscribers
  Anyone with an email account and a webcam can set up a YouTube channel. Amazingly, some of the most popular YouTube channels involve brief snippets of advice on topics like beauty and fashion. Other videos focus on products that the host loves. One woman who filmed daily videos about fingernail care tips from her bedroom garnered more than half of a million subscribers! By commenting and contributing to the complimentary YouTube channels with large followings, your brand will have the opportunity to gain exposure to groups it would not have otherwise connected with.

- Facebook Community Leaders

These individuals not only have a large number of Friends, but they may also manage groups or pages that could compliment your business. Developing a relationship with these people may be mutually beneficial as each brand will have increased exposure through cross-promotion. For example, if you manage a medical spa, you may find it helpful to develop a partnership with a manager of a busy hair salon's social media page who has lots of friends and followers.

- Industry-Specific Bloggers
Blogging is still a vital part of the interactive marketing mix, and it's one that millions of people are passionate about. Not only should you create and contribute to your own blog, but you should provide comments and your expertise to bloggers who might be willing to disseminate information about your business. Bloggers are constantly looking for fresh material. Guest authors add variety to their space and take some of the pressure off the blog's creator.

- Complementary Brands with Large Followings
Cross-promotion via interactive marketing with local brands that complement your products or services is a great way to broaden the reach for both brands. For example, our agency once took part in a promotional event for a surgeon who was partnering with a local celebrity dentist. This dentist just happened to have a massive social media following. By encouraging the dentist to post about the event, and the surgeon's name, this partnership allowed the surgeon to get his name out to thousands of people he otherwise would have never been able to reach.

Encouraging Participation on Social Media

Keeping things interactive is critical to the success of your internet marketing campaign. By encouraging participation on social media, you're taking control of the discussion about your brand.

To encourage participation and drive engagement, you should:

- **Ask Questions**. Asking your audience a question is a great way to get people talking about you. It's also a way to glean valuable information about how your brand is perceived by customers.
- **Run Contests.** According to a number of market research sources, a vast majority of social media users have created content to enter an online contest. Leverage this by encouraging your community to submit content as a contest entry form. For example, a Facebook giveaway entry form could request that users leave a comment stating the last time they visited your store, their favorite item to buy or why they love your brand so much.
- **Request Comments.** Sometimes simply asking people for their comments or suggestions about one of your products or services is all it takes to get a meaningful dialogue rolling.
- **Collect Recommendations.** A powerful way to supercharge your contests is to give people an entry into a raffle, or a coupon for one of your services, just for leaving a recommendation. Make sure to check with your attorney first…just in case. It is important that your actions on social media always be above-board, legal, and ethical. Some industries ban the encouragement of reviews altogether. So, when in doubt, check it out.

Engaged customers and potential customers can quickly get the word out about your business. And remember, these online contributions are written in stone, not pencil!

CHAPTER 5:

● ●

Traditional Marketing Vs. Social And Interactive Marketing

Advertising vs. Social Media

One of the challenges we face when discussing social media is getting people to accept that the world of marketing has changed. Communication methods have evolved quite a bit over time. Today it is much easier to have an effective, two-way dialog with your customers than ever before. Feedback can easily be solicited and provided, giving us all the opportunity to build and maintain meaningful business relationships.

As they say "out with the old, in with the new." While these new methods of communication have definitely made life easier, they have also made traditional marketing strategies obsolete. Simply put, many marketing paradigms just don't apply anymore.

Traditional Marketing Methods

For the sake of this discussion, we're going to call these older marketing methods traditional marketing methods to differentiate them from the newer digital marketing methods.

Traditional marketing methods include newspaper ads, *Yellow Pages*, billboards, flyers, and more.

We'll examine traditional marketing methods along several axes. These include:

- **Time**
  Traditional marketing methods tend to be transitory. A printed flyer or newspaper ad has a limited shelf life. As such, we can only hope that people are exposed to our promotions during that "live" period. When that edition is replaced by another – say, tomorrow's newspaper – then the promotion goes away. And once your vehicle for promotion has expired, your exposure drastically diminishes.

- **Business Model and Ownership**
  Many traditional marketing methods require consistent investment. This is what we call "pay to play." As the media buyer, you know you must continually pay for your ad to run, whether it's on TV, in newspapers or over the radio. Once you stop paying, the benefits dry up as well.

- **Frequency of Exposure**
  Some traditional ads (e.g. billboards) may make impressions on your audience several times per day. Others are "one and done," like radio, *Yellow Pages* and newspaper ads. You should consider your exposure and frequency of exposure before deciding whether something is worth adding to your marketing budget.

- **Audience**
  Audience is an important part of your advertising's effectiveness. Be wary of a magazine that says its distribution is in the millions. It is much better to pay attention to the quality of the audience

before determining whether that particular demographic is likely to buy from you. Many traditional marketing media avenues tend to deliver clientele that is highly focused geographically or highly focused by demographic, but rarely can they deliver both at the same time.

For the small business owner, typically traditional marketing methods do not carry an audience restriction. Most marketing campaigns using traditional methods carry indiscriminate targeting. Sophisticated marketers may segment their budget to target specifically (e.g. send marketing material targeting facelifts only to patients over the age of 55).

- **Quality of Communication**
  Make sure your message can be appropriately delivered through your chosen medium. Remember your marketing basics: you'll need to successfully deliver a compelling benefit, sense of urgency and call to action in one concise marketing message.

- **Effectiveness of Call to Action**
  When using traditional marketing methods, be sure you're requesting an action that the client can deliver. One of the biggest mistakes you can make as a business owner is spending tons of cash on an advertisement that includes a call to action that the client simply cannot complete. For this reason, website links and phone numbers are often ineffective bits of information on a roadside billboard, just as a long-winded URL or web address would be a poor fit for print media.

Digital Marketing

Digital media platforms, which include social media, online publishing and much more, have dramatically reduced the cost of publishing. As a business owner, you have access to the exact same tools as Coca-Cola or the Ford Motor Company. Therefore, with a little thought, you can deliver a world-class digital marketing campaign for minimal cost.

Some things to remember while you're planning this campaign…

Persistence of Message

Individual platforms may vary, but ads placed on different digital media will tend to have a much longer shelf life than their print counterparts. For the most part, you will have possession of your digital marketing campaign forever. Individual platforms will publish your content according to their own rules. Many social media platforms will give exposure to a simple message for a few minutes a day, but that message will live on forever in the digital archive. Self-publishing platforms like your blog, your website or an eBook distributor allow you to build up a large library of marketing content over time.

Business Model and Ownership

It sounds obvious, but you must understand how your platform works before you begin publishing content. Investing in a platform that you don't understand is never a good idea.

Platforms for Digital Marketing

Though you may have only one key marketing message with one key goal – get people in the door or on your website to buy things – you must realize that there are many different types of platforms where you can disseminate your message. All have their pros and cons, which mostly center on money and potential for exposure.

- **Advertising**. Ad space is like real estate: you want the most footage for the least amount of money…and you don't want to live near an annoying neighbor. Before you place your ad, make sure you understand whether your competitors' ads will also appear near your ads. This is a common tactic by aggressive marketers to capture new business.

  It is also important that you're both comfortable and confident in your abilities to utilize your chosen platform correctly before you begin publishing content. Spending a little more time understanding how people use a platform can help your "What's in it for me?" exercise to be more effective. This small investment of time and money can have a very strong effect on how your message will be displayed.

- **Freemium**. If your platform contains both a free and a premium (fee-based) version like LinkedIn, you should understand how a paid membership will affect your messaging. You should also compare how your messaging will appear for both categories of members. Note that in some cases, paid members (who may be the most valuable for your business) get an ad-free experience… which can reduce the value of your advertising investment.

Is Anything Really Free?

Many "free" online services have important rules about the sort of content that can be displayed. Understand how these rules work in order to avoid the complex web of copyright infringement.

Social media and digital self-publishing platforms generally allow you to have free access to your audience. Many platforms also include an automated filtering mechanism to stop users from generating a large quantity of poor-quality messaging, (you may know this as the spam that clogs up your inbox occasionally).

It's important to understand the applicable rules and laws regarding your platforms. For email and text (also known as Short Message System, or SMS) marketing, make sure you're familiar with CAN-SPAM laws or the equivalent in your country. For social networking websites, review their terms and conditions with your legal advisor to highlight areas of potential conflict.

Know Your Audience

Digital marketing is unique in that it allows you to select who will receive your message with very fine granularity. The most important part of this concept is permission. In digital marketing you have permission from your audience to send them messages. This occurs whenever an audience member – a potential or returning customer – becomes a fan of yours, chooses to follow your messaging streams or opts-in to your newsletter. Each of these actions gives you permission to send her messages.

These acts might seem tiny or insignificant, but the meaning and impact behind them is huge. Each person who performs one of these actions is essentially saying "send me your message, and I'm likely to act upon it."

With Great Privilege Comes Great Responsibility

As we just stated, things are rarely free. Your audience is no exception. Now that you've gotten their attention, you must use their time wisely. You've become a part of their networks now, and if you want to stay in that coveted space, you must treat them with both appreciation and respect.

Remember, you have a remarkable ability to impact your audience and to drive them to act based on your digital messaging. This current ability is much more significant than it ever was for any traditional marketing method. Building a smaller audience of loyal followers can result in much more action than reaching out to the masses in a generic way.

Take care that you do not abuse the permission your audience has given you, or it will be swiftly taken away.

If you are careless and waste this information, you will waste a valuable opportunity to engage with your audience while getting to know them better. Be sure to collect data on this audience in order to maximize the potential benefits from your social media marketing campaigns.

Switch It Up

Digital marketing lets you incorporate video, sound, images and text into your campaign. Though your audience may be targeted, each individual will have his or her own likes and preferences. Some will prefer reading. Others will enjoy watching videos. Fortunately, the internet allows you to disseminate your message in various forms. Be sure to use whichever media you deem appropriate in order to maximize your audience. Write a post, make a video, record audio, create a visual, etc.

We're not saying every, single message needs to be played out across all forms of media, but switching it up now and then allows you to inexpensively cast a wider net based on your audience's personal preferences. The more you interact with a person over their preferred method of communication, the easier it is to build a meaningful relationship with them.

Fun Fact

The time honored estimated cost of professional video production in the 1990s was "$1,000/minute." In 2013, semi-professional video production may be as low as $100/minute.

Keep It Simple (Stupid)

Simplicity is the goal of almost every marketing campaign. Why? Because, as we've mentioned before, you have limited time to capture someone's attention. If your message is unclear or bogged down with unnecessary jargon, a potential customer will simply move on. He's not going to sit there like Indiana Jones trying to decode whatever hidden treasure you're offering; it's far too easy for him to skip forward to funny pictures featuring puppies. Chances are, that photo probably contains 10 words or less – a few of which will be purposely misspelled – and the image was probably taken by an amateur using a smartphone. None of that matters, however, because the image has captured his attention. And it's not even selling anything!

Unless you're hocking puppies (the ethics of which is debatable), this meme-style marketing might not be for you. But that doesn't mean there isn't a lot to learn from its simplicity. Translated to the business world: if you make it easy for your audience to instantly understand your message, they will buy; when they do buy, they will spend more and buy more frequently.

An appropriately conceived digital marketing campaign will include a call to action that should have an immediate impact. Phrases like "Click here" or "Call us now!" provide a simple and immediate way for the audience to act upon your offer. Your message is now just one click away from being acted upon.

The mode of delivery is another important aspect of online marketing. Those viewing your message on a mobile device like a smartphone or tablet will not appreciate large amounts of text in your call to action. This is something that you shouldn't be doing anyway, but it becomes an even bigger issue when the viewing screen is reduced to 3 inches or less. Similarly, those reading your message on a laptop will not likely be motivated to get up and go to the mailbox if your call to action involves mailing in a rebate form. Know your audience, know their preferred online platforms and don't ask them to do something that's incompatible with those platforms.

Recruiting New Members

Recruitment in digital marketing tends to come from several sources, including advertising, search engine optimization and review-centric sites.

Advertising platforms require experimentation and testing. If you don't have either the expertise or time, then hiring an expert may be your shortest path to success. If you have the time to learn it, then treat it like any other marketing activity: test, measure, analyze, and repeat.

SEO is a fantastic way to obtain new clients. As mentioned above, customers will select you based on your web presence, so it's important that this adequately reflects your business, products and services. Search leaders like Google, Microsoft and Yahoo! are constantly fine-tuning their search algorithms to improve search results. Hire a trustworthy SEO advisor to ensure that your marketing budget is spent appropriately.

According to ReviewTrackers.com, peer-sourced review sites carry more credibility than search engine rankings as of 2013[7]. People turn to online review sites much more frequently than they have in the past. Many will even purposely seek out this information before booking a reservation, ordering a product online or visiting a store. For these reasons, review sites are a fantastic way to capture new clients. Staying up to date on what is posted about your business (and its competitors) should be a vital part of your new client acquisition strategy.

Turning Strangers into Friends (and Customers!)

Social media marketing is a fantastic conversion tool. Over time, your well-managed social media community will be the perfect audience for your new product and services announcements. This is because your social media community already likes and trusts you as a vendor. Use your social media

---

7   http://www.reviewtrackers.com/people-trust-customer-reviews-pro-critics/

campaign to strengthen that trust. Remember, this is the key audience that is most likely to want to hear about – and try out – your new products or services. Debuting new offerings over social media has peripheral effects, too. Your audience might feel that a particular product or service would be perfect for someone else within their trusted network of friends, family and colleagues. With any luck, they just might refer that person to you!

Paying Attention to Retention

Building barriers to prevent the competitor from chipping away at your customer base is at the very core of retention. For this reason, social media and interactive marketing can be a fantastic tool for retention.

The transparency of the World Wide Web turns digital marketing into one massive online magnifying glass for your business. Everything your business does is subject to scrutiny by the online community. Therefore, your brand must develop a strong sense of identity, and this sense must be at the basis of everything you communicate to your followers.

Your identity is composed of the business' mission, vision and personality (MVP). A properly selected MVP is vital. It should be designed to attract and retain your target clientele.

Zappos.com is one company that has an excellent MVP. This identity permeates throughout every branding message it sends. While the exact secrets to the online shoe and apparel powerhouses' success lie with its founder, Tony Hsieh, a few generalities can be gleaned from simply analyzing its business model.

Here are a few of the simple values that we believe are core to Zappos' success:

- Zappos competes on service, not price.
- Hsieh insists that employees have just a little bit of "weirdness," as opposed to insisting that everyone conform to a company mold. In

fact, one of its published core values reads "At Zappos, we're always creating fun and a little weirdness!"

- Hsieh talks often about delivering the "wow factor" to his customers. He is focused on the ways in which Zappos can over deliver on what it promises. Another core value reads "Deliver WOW through service!"

More information about Zappos.com and its success can be found in Hsieh's book, *Delivering Happiness*. We can tell you firsthand that it contains some fascinating insights into the thought process behind building a personality that supports a brand's national success.

Developing Your Own MVP

When your business' MVP infiltrates everything in your operation, from your front desk to your online presence, you'll know you're prepared to successfully enter the world of interactive marketing. Simply put, your interactive marketing campaign will reflect your MVP. Your target clientele will be attracted to this MVP, and you'll begin to build that community of loyal customers.

This is where retention comes in. In essence, you've built a better mousetrap. You've baited this trap with a particular flavor of cheese, and now your basement is swarming with mice that have developed an affinity for this type of cheese. Step 1 is understanding exactly what about your cheese your mice enjoyed. Step 2 is making that cheese easily and abundantly available. With these two problems solved, there should be a constant stream of mice beating a path to your door.

Indeed, it's very clear that the world has changed. Customers, technology and even culture have changed with it. Guess what that means? It means that marketing has also been forced to evolve over the years. The days of throwing up a billboard and waiting for your clients to show have passed. Your new mantra for success is based on knowing your identity, being transparent and vocal about your brand and consistently delivering on your promises.

CHAPTER 6:

●●

Marketing State Of The Union

As we've discussed, the recent digital revolution has forever changed the landscape of marketing. Small business owners now have tools available to them that would have been featured in a Sci-fi story as recently as the mid-'90s. By the late-'90s, these technologies were well on their way!

Unfortunately, many businesses are still afraid, or don't understand, or are afraid they don't understand these new technologies (which are not so new anymore). Business owners with this mindset typically engage in what we call "comfort zone" marketing.

Their efforts tend to include:

- On-site: signage, coupons, flyers
- Billboards: off-site signage in complementary businesses or roadside
- TV and radio: ads aired on both media, which are still effective for some businesses today
- Websites: official web presence marked by your domain/business name.

As you can see, interactive and social media marketing is often outside the small business owner's comfort zone. As the new millennium progressed, innovations in mobile computing and interactive marketing made low-cost digital marketing possible for the small business owner. Even with a significant reduction in the barriers to entry, many small business owners remained steadfast in their apprehension surrounding the digital marketing space.

What makes this issue even worse is that many of the brave souls who attempted to enter the interactive and social media space failed most of the time.

Why Small Businesses Fail at Interactive and Social Media Marketing

Small businesses that enter the world of social media marketing tend to fail because:

- They apply the old maxims of advertising
- Pitching far too often
- They apply old metrics of advertising success
- Audience size (number of Likes)
- Number of impressions (reach)

Pitching too often is generally a major turn-off to social media users. Think about it. This approach is not customer-centric. Constant advertising does not fit within the potential customer's network or motivations for utilizing these online platforms…connecting and socializing. Constant promotion can result in a loss of followers and damage to your brand's reputation. If not presented appropriately to your community, your business can look like an aggressive used car salesman!

To counteractive this potential perception, many small business owners will simply stick their heads in the sand and avoid social and interactive media altogether. As we're sure you're aware by now, these business owners are doing themselves a huge disservice. They are ignoring potentially valuable market insight that could be used to improve their product or service!

Applying the incorrect metrics is just wrong thinking. Too many small business owners get caught up in the arms race of 'fans and followers', focusing only on the size of their social media community and not on the revenue it's generating for their business. Remember, banks do not accept Facebook Likes as an appropriate form of deposit!

Fun Fact

Did you know that according to a poll done by MedAesthetics magazine, nearly half of all medical aesthetic practices recently surveyed said they have NO social media presence?!

That's right. MedEsthetics magazine recently surveyed nearly 600 medical aesthetic practices, and 42 percent said they do not have a social media presence. In fact, one industry insider was even quoted as saying that more than half of the offices he works with do not even bother collecting email addresses!

Just as your consumer base might be composed of people of all ages, we assume that the people reading this book might be as well. We're aware that there is likely a generational divide. A few of you may embrace social media and online marketing very enthusiastically. Others are likely terrified or confused by it. Some still might not be convinced that it's worth the investment. If you're in the latter two groups, it's more important than ever that you keep reading!

Yes, every generation has a different mindset regarding marketing. This is simply the way we were brought up to think, that there is a zero-sum game in advertising. As an example, and to illustrate this concept, say you're driving down the road and are presented with two billboards: one for a restaurant and one for a gas station. These companies have very little time to grab your attention. Because there are two billboards, they're also competing for this small window of opportunity. In this case, if the restaurant had the catchier graphic, it is possible that the gas station billboard may not have been seen. There was a winner and a loser. Thus, the zero-sum game.

It is no longer enough to just put your message in the faces of potential customers, as in the billboard example. In the new space of interactive and social media marketing, you have to *attract* people to your brand. More specifically, your brand has to be *attractive* to your following. This is essential because you have to motivate people to actively Like your page on Facebook, leave that +1 on Google+ or retweet you on Twitter.

To create this relationship, you must be interesting. Undoubtedly, one of the most interesting things a person will find about your brand's social media page is the promise of exclusive discounts. People have enough Friends on social media whom they know in real life. If they are making the effort to connect with your brand, you'd better demonstrate what kind of value they can expect to get out of this relationship.

Promoting Your Products and Services

One of the major questions you may have at this point is whether you should mention your medical aesthetic practice's products/procedures in your social media posts.

In short, yes. Sparingly.

Take a deep breath before you act on the instinct to tell everyone how wonderful you, your products and your services are. Remember, your followers have allowed you to enter a very special zone on social media that is mostly reserved for friends and family.

More likely than not, they've chosen to connect with your brand because they understand there will be some sort of special offer you'll make available to only to followers. However, if you start spamming your audience or inundating them about how great you are, they are likely to tune out or, worse, hit "unsubscribe."

To understand where we're coming from, you only have to look as far as your own social media networks (if you have any, that is). If you have personal accounts on sites like Facebook, Google+ and Twitter, you probably have a friend, relative or acquaintance who is all too eager to spread the word about their new role as a Mary Kay, Avon, Amway or Pampered Chef consultant. *Come to my party! Spread the word to your friends! Contact me for all your kitchen needs!*

Annoying, isn't it? What they're basically saying is: *let me invade your personal social media space with my own agenda, wants and needs!* While you might be happy for a close friend who secures a new job or scores a promotion uses social media to announce this news, those good feelings can quickly sour once you realize they want something from you.

It's just like that annoying friend or family member who calls you only when they need something. Eventually, you're likely to step back from the relationship, reduce contact, and perhaps even delete their messages or screen their calls from here on out. No one likes to feel used, especially in this fast-paced world. Our time is valuable, and no one wants to think they have to spend it listening to the requests, demands and pleas of others.

Do NOT be "that guy."

We know you have a business to grow. And that telling you to "get your butt on social media," while saying in the same breath "but not too much" can feed right back into the confusion that might have initially caused you to buy this book. Fear not. It's all about balance.

This can all be done by adhering to the Social 80/20. The definition of this concept says that for every promotional message you disseminate you should put out at least four no-strings-attached, non-promotional messages. This should amount to 80 percent "give," for every 20 percent of "ask." This should be simple enough to follow: you offer a discount, followed by a link to an industry-related news story, a question that will pique your followers' interests, a fun fact related to your industry and maybe a random thought related to something relevant that's happening right now in pop culture, etc.

Once in a while we are asked whether a business owner can subtly slip in a discussion about his products or services into the non-promotional posts. It can be done, but this strategy comes with significant risks. Your customers are smart people, and most are likely to see right through veiled advertising.

Say you own a laser skin care center, and you want to put out non-promotional messaging about lasers in general. Perhaps you have a new spa that carries a line of products containing botanical ingredients. It is possible for you to put out good educational material on the benefits of these procedures in a manner that your audience will not view as promotional or self-serving.

To be successful, however, you must appeal to the higher-order benefit that people are seeking by getting laser procedures or buying a skin care product in the first place. Namely, they want to feel better about themselves!

This means you must...

- abstain from placing the brand names of products or devices within your non-promotional posts.
- refrain from tying whatever products contain these botanical ingredients to any promotions you are running.
- ensure that the theme of the post focuses on one's overall health and wellness.

Advertising's Role

As a business owner, you will always have the need to cast a net over your city or targeted demographic to see what you catch. As such, advertising is always going to be part of your strategy.

Interactive and social media will play equally critical roles as they motivate people to visit you more often and increase the lifetime value of each customer relationship. This, in turn, significantly drives up your advertising program's Return on Investment (ROI).

Without a doubt, some level of advertising will always be needed for your business to attract new customers who were otherwise unfamiliar with it. Interactive and social media marketing will ensure that your hard work and financial investment in new customer acquisition does not go to waste.

How Does Your Practice Rate on Interactive and Social Media?

Truth is, there is a bewildering array of social media marketing outlets available today. To mount an effective marketing campaign, you have to choose the right media and deliver the proper content to that media.

Your social marketing report card from Total Social Solutions is a great first step. The report is a pointed evaluation of your past performance on social networks and draws on more than 20 years of sales and marketing experience as we evaluate your practice's strategy.

The report card serves three important functions:

1. Focus

   The report card focuses on the social networks that matter. Thus, your performance on Friendster is not going to be an item of discussion.

2. Depth

   The report card looks beyond participation and into the quality of this participation. We know the types of activities that are proven to bring results, and the report card can give you this insight.

3. Relevance

   Our team is specifically looking for activities that are known to work within the medical practice industry. Our results are designed for you, and rate your past activities against our best practices.

CHAPTER 7:

●●

Keys To Success On Interactive
And Social Media Marketing

If you can follow these simple steps, you'll be able to execute a high-ROI social media marketing campaign that will deliver more business for years to come.

Graphic and Interactive Design

Many social media marketing platforms interweave your content with others, making it even more difficult for you to stand out against the swarms of baby pictures, vacation photos and pithy celebrity comments streaming across your potential customers' screens.

We have an evolutionary prioritization algorithm built into our psyches. It stems from survival skills on the African savannahs: focus on the wrong thing and you may quickly end your chance to reproduce. Choosing the right thing and you can increase your chances for food, reproduction opportunities and, essentially, survival.

Our brains prioritize our environment as follows:

- **High.** Moving images, this could be a threat, it could be dinner. Either way, pay attention, brain!

- **Medium.** Still images, this is probably not a threat, but it could still be dinner. Let's pay attention, but only if we're not being chased by a pack of hyenas.
- **Low.** Text, this was never really viewed as a threat, or as an opportunity to reproduce, so it gets pushed to the back of the processing queue.

Within social media, we've seen an eerily opposite evolution of capabilities. When people began interacting on the relatively young internet, they did so on all-text message boards. Users quickly began generating text-only art to entertain and amuse, creating images from characters on their keyboard. Social media platforms began to support imagery and, eventually, video streaming.

Naturally, compelling graphics and consistent branding will be tremendous assets to your social media marketing campaign. Using video and still images can dramatically increase your effectiveness.

Here are some very simple guidelines for posting visual content on your social media spaces.

First, the Do's. Please…

- Enforce Brand Consistency
  All around the world, you recognize a McDonald's restaurant when you see one. While they may serve seaweed fries in Asia, and the McRib in the U.S., the signature golden arches remain the same. In the same way, as a business owner you want your followers to *always* know when they see your content. An easy way to do this is to make sure your branding is always present. Keep your logo and our name consistent whenever you're marketing for yourself.

- Use Videos
  High-quality video is becoming increasingly less expensive to

record and produce. In addition, video is a compelling way to communicate your value to your users.

- Show Them How the Sausage is Made
There is an enormous amount of professionally produced entertainment on television that does nothing more than show people how things are done. Take advantage of your customers' natural curiosity and educate them on your business processes. This might include your shipping department, your factory or a different type of service you offer. This is a great way to showcase all aspects of your business and, thus, a fantastic conversion tool.

- Pander to the Masses
If people love to see pictures of puppies and babies – and if it's consistent with your brand – then absolutely give them what they want and deliver pictures of puppies and babies. It works.

- Understand How Different Platforms Display Your Content
Different social media platforms will display your content in different ways. How a message appears on a desktop computer can vary wildly when compared to a smartphone. Make sure you realize what your content will look like across the technology platforms before you publish it.

And please do not...

- Steal Content
Intellectual property law is racing to keep up with digital communications, but the underlying principles have not changed. Make sure any content you use is properly licensed. If you don't, you not only risk penalties to your social space, but litigation as well. It's legal, moral and practical to do it the right way.

- Forget About the Different Viewing Platforms
Screen sizes are constantly changing. Your audience is likely viewing your content on screens that range from 4 inches to 52 inches. You must be keenly aware of how your visual content displays.

- Neglect Your Marketing Basics
The content you create should follow basic marketing principles in order to deliver high-ROI results.

Community Involvement

In social media, as in life, it can truly take a village. Here is a list of your most important community members.

Staff

The first part of your community is your staff. Any important underlying message behind your interactive marketing campaign should be "we're people too." Successful campaigns integrate your team into the business. Putting a face (or many faces) to a company reminds your customers that your business is a team of likable, enthusiastic people.

Inexpensive digital media production tools like smartphones that produce high-quality images and videos make it easy to involve your staff in your campaign. This is something you should definitely foster throughout the office. Encourage your team to get involved through contests, photos of social activities and more. It will help your followers understand that your company has heart. That these messages aren't coming from a bunch of emotionless androids.

Your social media campaign will always have its roots in your brick-and-mortar facilities. Think about the different places where your clients interact with your business.

Let's take, for example, a plastic surgeon. She might say her clients communicate with her business either over the phone, in her facility (in the reception area, when checking out and paying bills), by email, and through her website.

A strategy for on-site support of your interactive marketing campaign that addresses these points will include the following:

For every phone call, if a person is placed on hold, then play audio highlighting the benefits of social network and email newsletters. During the course of regular phone customer service, require your phone personnel to collect email addresses for every call. Finally, make you're your phone personnel are trained to ask if clients are connected with the business on social networks, and to tout the benefits of being connected.

A similar process should be followed for in-office visits. Make sure that every patient is asked for email information with every office visit. The same message that we gave to phone callers about the benefits of being connected on social networks can also be delivered in the office. Because the office is typically a place where people have to wait, encourage clients to connect to a Wi-Fi network to review videos of current procedures or specials.

Don't neglect your email marketing campaign. Email is pervasive, and an incredibly effective way to connect with your patients. Since you've collected email addresses from your patients, take advantage of this to follow up with patients. Make sure you ask particularly happy patients to share their experience online either with their social networks or on review websites.

For your website, make sure you remind people how they can stay connected with you.

When you craft your campaign, brainstorm with your staff about other ways in which your day-to-day operations can support your marketing goals.

Vendors

The second part of your community is your vendors. No one is more invested in your success than your vendors. Make it a point to reach out to them individually and ask them for any tips they may have as to how you can better market your business and, therefore, their products and services.

At least once per year, you should ask your vendors what other businesses in your space are doing that is particularly effective. Ask what kind of help they can offer you for marketing. Even better, if the vendor is familiar with your business, ask him what he would do differently if he were in your shoes. This type of environmental scanning is a critical part of turning your vendors into partners that will help you grow your business.

Clientele

Finally, the most important part of your community is your clientele. With their enthusiastic participation, you are empowering them to become your brand's advocates. Sharing your success with them and giving them credit for their helping turns them into your teammates and unofficial cheerleaders for success.

Here are some simple tips on how to treat your community:

- Share your success, but *always* give credit to the clients for helping get you there.
- When possible, legal and appropriate, highlight the success of your customers as well. For example, if you have a regular customer that is receiving a community award, use your platform to support that person (with their permission). Make that customer's success everyone else's success!

- Set aside time on a daily or weekly basis to engage and interact with your community on social media spaces.
- Coordinate real-world events that buoy your community. Support a charity, hold an event. Just be sure to emphasize that these are "giving back" events. Resist the urge to turn them into massive sales channels.

Retail Margins

Internet marketing and sales changed the retail business permanently. Finally, savvy shoppers were given tools that allow them to compare brick-and-mortar pricing with an entire world of vendors. As a result, competitive business owners have slashed margins to be paper-thin online. Competition is stiff; there is always someone who is willing to undercut your price by just a little in order to win away your customers.

Let's take a real world example. Imagine I'm looking to buy tires in Phoenix. Google tells me I have almost 500,000 results to choose from. That's far too many choices for me, so I'll hop over to an online review site and see what I can find there.

Now I'm down to just 80 results. That's much more manageable. If I sort by "highest-rated," I can see at least 10 options that are considered simply excellent by that establishment's actual customers. A little smart shopping shows me I can buy tires in town at a price that cannot be matched on the internet. It's very challenging to compete with an incredibly inexpensive package by a top-rated vendor.

If you're competing on price, you simply can't win. Price competition is a lose-lose proposition. You'll wind up cutting your margins to the bone. Ironically, with this strategy, your biggest fear is success. If you earn too many customers who are accustomed to your bargain-rate pricing, you may wind up working around the clock while still not making enough profit to pay the rent. "We'll make it up on volume" is a good way to earn a tiny profit margin and lots of headaches.

Why is this? It's because it's very difficult to raise prices on customers. Once you condition them to pay a certain amount, you risk damaging a relationship by increasing that amount. If you've captured a customer because they see you as a low-cost provider, then raising the perception of your value – and the price you can command – is very difficult.

Work Less, Earn More

Rather than work twice as hard to capture borderline profitable customers, why not work less and earn more?

Don't cast a wide net to catch small, unprofitable fish. Instead, put a little bait on the hook and catch the whale you actually want. Manually go through your network and select a few people whom you believe might be influential. If you can't find any, consider your local community and select some people with loud voices.

Now the next question, obviously, is how do you know if someone's influential? Easy. Determine the size of a customer's network. View her social networking activity. Try a few online reputation tools like Klout or LinkedIn, and see how her reputation stacks up. See how often she posts to Yelp, if at all. Come across pictures of her with the local school board? Or perhaps at a charity run? She's probably influential and at least somewhat involved in the larger community. With a little reconnaissance, you can quickly determine which of your customers holds influence within his or her networks.

Once you've identified these people, offer them something really special. Something really compelling.

Examples include:

- A free procedure for a friend if she accompanies her to her next appointment
- A free tour of the facility, followed by a special treatment
- A free wine/lunch/dinner voucher when she schedules (and shows up to) her next appointment

Once a potential influencer comes in for her appointment, make sure your staff knows that they should:

- Give her the white glove treatment
- Ensure her wait is short
- Follow up with her via phone or email

Here's the good news: you'll have an easy time selling free. Free really gets people through the door in droves. But you're not done yet. Free can't do all the work for you.

Once you get her through the door, it's up to you to make sure you:

- Do a great job.
- Have a plan to convert a non-paying customer into a paying customer. Be honest but discreet about your methods. Tell your customer you believe she's an influencer (flattery always works) and that you're trying to build your online reputation. Encourage her to share an honest review of her experience with her network.
- Ask that customer if she wants to book a follow-up appointment after her procedure is complete.
- Remind the customer that your best way to get new business is through referrals. It's worth noting here that paying for referral can have legal consequences; please consult with your attorney before putting such a policy in place.

If you deliver excellent customer service, you just might have captured a customer for life. With any luck – and a couple of good references – you may convert a few of that customer's friends as well. The value of an influential new customer (or two) is much, much greater than zero.

Messaging

There are two types of messaging on your interactive media: promotional and non-promotional.

As we mentioned, at least 80 percent of the content you post should be fun, relevant, social, interesting, etc. In other words, not a business pitch. The remaining 20 percent can be devoted to showcasing deals and crisp, well defined calls to action for your audience.

Non-Promotional Messaging

Non-promotional messaging is a critical part of your marketing campaign. It also goes hand-in-hand with the community-building we discussed earlier. In order to lead a vocal, active community, you need to foster whatever values your business stands for.

Say you run a local camping and firearms supply store. We can assume that customers might be interested in Second Amendment debates, wilderness preservation and information about local hunting conditions. You can become a leader in this community by delivering relevant, timely information and by fostering constructive discussions on these topics.

Over time, you'll accumulate community members that are interested in these topics, thus identifying yourself as an authority and trusted advisor on all (or at least the most timely and relevant) matters concerning camping and firearms activities.

Note that none of these efforts involve pitching your products or services. Your community members are generally aware that you run a for-profit business. For your non-promotional content, being at the forefront of interesting discussions is often enough

This is also where you can add personality to your content. The world has spoken, and time and again we have learned that some topics simply bring out great positive interactions.

There are a few easy ways to develop content from the office that will provide personality for your business. Post pictures of your office staff (this encourages their social networks to get engaged. Post pictures of beautiful or famous scenes from your neighborhood or surrounding area. This could include a nearby park, favorite lunch spot or even unique tourist attraction. Finally, don't be afraid to pander to your patients' inner nurturing instincts. Post pictures of babies and puppies. We know, we know, again with the babies and puppies. What can we say? Cute sells. If someone in the office has a young child or particularly photogenic pet, feel free to post those pictures online with an appropriately fun caption. These always lend your business personality.

It's very important to manage your social community with professional leadership. Avoid controversial topics and polarizing issues. A little personality can also go a long way when integrated into your posts. Add a little color or local flair to your already useful content and watch it shine!

Promotional Messaging

Promotional content is the 20 percent that turns social media into social media marketing.

When doing this, always remember to:

- Follow the marketing basics in Chapter 3 to ensure your messaging is effective.
- Never oversaturate your audience with "deals, deals, deals!" Avoid the temptation to turn off your audience by turning into a giant, needy billboard for your brand.
- Measure the results from every promotion…and learn from them. Marketing is a never-ending learning process. Over time you'll develop great knowledge about what works and what doesn't.

Focus on return. In order to capture return, you must have a compelling promotion, an attentive and real audience, and a well-crafted message. If you deliver all three, then you will see return.

CHAPTER 8:

• •

Supercharging Your Interactive And
Social Media Marketing Efforts

As we mentioned early on, social media is just one area within the bigger, ever-evolving space of interactive marketing.

Not only are these platforms effective, but they are relatively inexpensive now when compared to a few years ago. While social media is a wonderful tool, the harsh reality is that a fair amount of your online community will *not* be active on these platforms. Therefore, it is critical to the future health of your business to reach out to your customers by whatever means they most desire. These alternative means tend to also be low cost while providing a high ROI.

Some of these non-social-media-based-but-nevertheless-important interactive marketing options include:

1. Email campaigns
2. Mobile device applications (apps)
3. Connecting online with VIPs
4. Review sites

1. Email Campaigns

Email may be more than 40 years old[8], but it's still an incredibly powerful medium for small business owners. However, it is imperative that you follow these three directives to ensure your email campaign is effective and profitable.

I. Track Performance

It is amazing how many of our agency's clients tell us they've been emailing their customers for years, but have *never* tracked the performance of an email campaign. Like any investment you make in your business, it is critical to have a well-defined set of goals, as well as steps to achieve those goals. With those goals in mind, tracking performance across the key metrics is mandatory.

II. Drive Recruitment

Email has been ubiquitous and widespread since the late '90s. Even so, many small business owners do *not* regularly collect emails from customers or sales leads. The good news is it's easier than ever to build your business' email database today.

III. Keep Your Brand Consistent

Like anything in digital marketing, it is important that your brand have a consistent look, feel and personality. This is imperative when it comes to email, as this may be one of the only interactions that some of your customers will have with your brand over the course of a month.

---

8   http://www.marketingtechblog.com/infographic-the-history-of-email/

Simple Ways to Drive Recruitment

- **Ask.** Simply ask a customer for his or her email address the next time they visit your store. You should assume that some of your customers will want to hear that they'll gain access to attractive incentives in exchange for their email. Others will want the reassurance that you're not planning to sell their information to third parties.

- **Capture Leads on Your Website.** Have your website vendor prepare a small lead capture tool on your homepage. This short form should be as minute as possible and should aim to capture the visitor's name, email address and phone number. Make sure you remember the WIIFM ("What's in it for them?"), and promise them access to exclusive information or discounts for insiders only.

- **Utilize On-site Signage.** Attractive signage around your office should highlight the benefits of being on your business' email list. It should also tell them how they can easily sign up for this list.

- **Make Your Forms Uniform**. All of your forms should require – or at least request – that your customers leave their email address.

- **Incentivize Staff.** Encourage your staff to collect emails from customers who frequent your business. A fun contest with prize money for the staff member who collects the most (legitimate) emails in a month is a great way to build your database while keeping employees motivated!

Building Your Brand's Consistency

Consistently reviewing your emails will ensure that you're not only communicating your brand's key visual attributes, but conveying to your audience where they should turn for information about your company and industry insights.

Visually, your email should feature:

- **Colors.** Make sure the color palate in your email is consistent with the one on your website and social media spaces. Generally speaking, the key driver for your e-communications color palate should be your brand's logo.
- **Fonts.** Pick a font that's identical or at least similar to the one in your logo. You may need to accept a close match, as some email platforms do not offer a rich database of fonts to choose from. Just do the best you can.
- **White space.** Less is oftentimes more. If your brand is one that has a clean, modern feel, you'll want to include plenty of white space. If your brand is colorful, lively and active, you may want your content to outweigh the white space. It is your brand. You should have an intuitive sense about what will work best for you and your customers.
- **Imagery.** People love pictures and videos. Luckily, these are very easy to include in emails. Pick imagery that you feel will resonate with your target. Or, show off your brand's personality through a short video clip imported from your YouTube channel!
- **Structure.** Develop consistent departments for your regular emails. Much like a newspaper has different sections for different content, your readers should know where to look for the information they want when your email hits their inbox.

2. Mobile Device Applications

Picture life without your smartphone. Pretty hard, huh? Smartphones have become an integral part of our everyday lives. Mobile technology in general touches nearly every part of our world. Small business owners have a powerful opportunity in the area of mobile device applications to get their brand literally into the hands (or purses, or pockets) of their target consumers.

The modern concept of a mobile app became mainstream in July 2008 when Apple debuted the App Store on iTunes. It was launched just one day before the iPhone 3G. In its first five years, the App Store made 1 million third-party applications available for sale and/or download. Competitive platforms immediately sprung up from other companies to support devices like Google's Android or Amazon's Kindle Fire, and with good cause. Mobile applications are big business. Juniper Research estimates that by 2014, the direct and indirect revenues from the sale of mobile apps will total $25 billion.

Is a Mobile Application Right for My Business?

YES!

Apps are the perfect augment to any business that is looking to develop a closer and more profitable relationship with its customers.

Here are a few of the reasons why apps are the perfect way for small businesses to keep in touch with their customer base.

- **Mobile is Everywhere.** It seems like everyone has a smartphone nowadays. In July 2012, Nielsen reported that 54.9 percent of U.S. mobile subscribers owned a smartphone.
- **People Love Smartphones.** There's no denying the seemingly unbreakable bond between people and their smartphones. We've become so besotted with these phones, that many states have even passed laws prohibiting their use while driving. As a society, we can't put them down!

  Instant Connectivity. People have a Pavlovian response when their smartphone chirps, indicating the arrival of a new message. Your brand has an opportunity to deliver value to your audience, and that audience can't wait to hear from you!

Some members of our team recently visited a beautiful medical spa business in the Southwest. The office had attractive marketing materials strategically placed throughout its space. It even featured some high-tech educational equipment in the waiting room. During the brief visit, our team members reported that about 10 clients passed through the waiting room. Their stays ranged from 2 minutes to 6 minutes. So how many of these clients looked through the high-tech educational materials?

None.

Instead, all 10 spent their time in the waiting room browsing through their smartphones. We can't say for sure what they were looking at, but they certainly weren't paying attention to the expensive marketing materials that were all over the place!

This medical spa missed a *massive* selling opportunity. The customers were already on site, were open to receiving additional news from outside sources and were in the perfect position to receive positive messaging from the brand. In response, our firm began offering a mobile app that our clients can use to further their relationships with customers.

Fun Fact

DID YOU KNOW…that a successful app for a medical aesthetic practice should include the following?!

- Push (pop-up) messaging to help you rapidly fill open appointment slots
- Messaging functionality to include text and photo transmission
- Direct links to your blog
- Direct links to your review sites to encourage more positive reviews
- A tool to request appointments

A Word of Caution About Vanity Apps

Do NOT develop a mobile app for vanity reasons!

Any investment in your business should be directed at delivering measured business improvements to your overall operation. All too often, our firm has seen clients purchase apps simply to 'keep up with the Joneses'. Some of these apps do not deliver functionality and suck additional revenue from the business.

Before you decide to create a mobile application for your business, make sure you have a rough idea of which revenue-generating customer actions you are trying to drive. Focusing on this will ensure a positive return on your marketing and technology investment.

3. Connecting Online with VIPS

Yelp and interactive platforms like it are generally categorized as social media review sites. This means Yelp and similar platforms allow users to set up personal profiles and connect with others through a variety of different methodologies.

The popularity of social media review sites has caught fire over the past several years. Throughout the 2000s, a number of pure-play review sites popped up that gave consumers real reviews from the business' customers. These reviews provided an objective look into the business' overall performance, allowing a prospective customer to compare and contrast before making the best possible decision.

There was just one problem...many of these sites allowed users to leave anonymous reviews.

During the early to mid-2000s, CitySearch led the way in the review site marketplace. However, the biggest criticism of this site (and of others during the same period) was that it did not have any sort of filtering system in place to discourage unscrupulous business owners from:

- Leaving positive reviews for their own business
- Leaving poor reviews for competing businesses

As a result, the review sites grew in size, but became less useful as time went on and fake reviews proliferated. Industry experts recognize that this issue will continue indefinitely, with some estimates stating that about 15 percent of all online reviews will be fake by 2015[9]. The fact is, there will always be people looking to cheat the system. Fortunately, some advances in technology have reduced the likelihood that the fake review will skew the genuine public perception of top-rated businesses in your area.

When Yelp launched in the Bay Area in 2004, it stood out from other review sites because it forced users to leave reviews under their own profile, using their true identity. While this was novel to the market, the big breakthrough with Yelp was how it incorporated a proprietary review filter that quite literally weeds out reviews that Yelp suspected may not be legitimate, as well as those that were likely solicited by business owners.

Still, the Yelp filter is far from perfect. It's in a constant state of improvement. The algorithm used within this filter is a closely guarded secret, much like Google's search algorithm, but some things *are* known about how Yelp's filter works.

Yelp's review filter is likely to *favor* reviews:

- From active, or Elite Yelp users
- From users who add multimedia, such as photos

---

9   http://techcrunch.com/2012/09/17/reality-check-10-15-of-social-media-fans-likes-and-reviews-will-be-fake-by-2014-says-gartner/

Yelp's review filter is likely to filter *out* reviews:

- Left from the IP address associated with the business being reviewed
- From first-time Yelpers who do not remain active

Yelp also maintains a Terms of Service that is well defined, transparent and public. The terms are in place to minimize the chance that improper reviews will be left on the site. Nonetheless, many business owners are routinely frustrated as the powerful Yelp filter can, in fact, filter out legitimate reviews left by happy customers.

Not one to be left out of the social review game, Google made two separate attempts to purchase Yelp in the late '00s. CEO Jeremy Stoppelman declined both offers before taking the company public in March 2012.

Determined to be the leading provider of the social review sites, Google responded by building a platform off its already popular Google Maps product. The short-lived Google Places launched in 2011 before being converted to an offshoot of Google's social network, Google+. From then on, this product became known as Google+ Local.

Marissa Meyer, former vice president of Google's product management and current CEO of Yahoo!, once described Google+ Local as "an amazing local-mobile-social moment."

She probably did this for a few reasons:

- **Social Integration.** This new product integrated the power of Google's massive database with its Google+ social network
- **Zagat.** After its attempts to acquire Yelp were denied, Google purchased the popular subscription-only review publication for $151 million
- **Mobile.** Google Maps' usage is split 50/50 between mobile and desktop users. Mobile usage of GMaps is expected to rise significantly. This is important for Google+ Local, as advertisers will now be able to pinpoint potential customers on a geo-specific basis

Consumers place credibility in reviews that come from the masses. If you can put your ego aside and "face the music," so to speak, review sites like Yelp, Google+ Local and others are a great way to not only gain clients, but important information about the true quality of your operations.

4. Review Sites

There is one other opportunity you have as a small business owner when it comes to these social media review sites. That's advertising. Advertising on social media review sites is a controversial topic due to the inherent conflict of interest that comes when money exchanges hands on a site where reviews should remain unbiased. However, your business does have the opportunity to break through the noise on these sites and take advantage of some advertising opportunities.

For example, Yelp offers small business owners a few different ways to get the word out to prospective customers.

Some of its advertising products include:

- Enhanced profiles
- Pay-per-impression (a view of the advertisement by a user)
- Pay-per-click

Yelp also launches other advertising products in local markets all the time, so the list actually extends far beyond what's listed above. If your business has a low rating (3.5 out of 5 stars or below), advertising on Yelp is probably not the best strategy for you. This is a sign that your time and money is better spent on your internal operations and customer service, rather than simply "throwing money at the problem."

If your business has a good rating (4 stars or above), then advertising on social media review sites can be incredibly powerful and profitable. In fact, some of our clients are realizing a monthly ROI of more than 6,000 percent just by utilizing the strategic tools available through these advertising platforms!

Like it or not, crowd-sourced review sites are here to stay. More specifically, social-driven review sites are here to stay. They will only grow over time. Sticking your head in the sand and ignoring these platforms because you feel burned by a few bad reviews is not an option for the long-term vitality of your business. Instead, you must actively manage your presence…and people's perceptions of your business.

CHAPTER 9:

···

Let's Get Started

Congratulations! You now have all the information you need to develop a winning interactive marketing plan for your small business. Now, you're ready to hit the ground running…

Build Your Plan

When building your own plan for profitable interactive marketing, it is critical that you understand a few key facts.

- Begin building your community now (not later)
- Focus on customer relationships
- Realize and appreciate that interactive and social media are here to stay; they will eventually become a part of all our online experiences

Options to Getting Started

In the beginning of this book, we spoke about the importance of methodical and deliberate planning. Many small business owners think strategic and tactical planning is only for the big corporate entities. This could *not* be further from the truth. Especially when many small business owners assume all of the financial risk.

When it comes to getting your interactive marketing plan off the ground, you have three options:

1. Do it yourself, using this book as a guide
2. Hire in-house talent to manage your daily efforts and provide metrics
3. Contact a professional agency

Regardless of which option you choose, the checklist below will provide the key to your organization's execution and performance monitoring.

Checklist for Success: Interactive and Social Marketing for YOUR Business

- **Choose Success**. It sounds simple, but many business owners never get past the first critical step, which is to *choose* to be successful. You have to make a conscious decision to *want* to succeed in the arenas of interactive and social marketing. If you've read this far into the book, odds are you're ready for Step 2.
- **Be Active**. Success in anything does not come easy, it always requires work. Now that you've made the decision to be successful, it's important you recognize that interactive and social marketing is not something you can simply throw money at. You and your staff must be involved. Interactive marketing is just that...interactive.
- **Select Your Team Carefully**. Unless you have unlimited time on your hands (hint: you don't), you will need help with these efforts. You must not take a flippant stance toward interactive and social media. You cannot afford to say "it's just a Facebook post." These platforms are serious business because they *are* the face of your business for so many customers. Place your interactive and social

media program into the hands of a professional who can help you develop and execute upon a strategic marketing plan. This is vital to the overall health and success of your business. Look to appoint a social captain or interactive captain who will ultimately take responsibility for your program and report back to you with its performance progress.

- **Position Yourself.** If you want your customers to know how you differ from your competition, then you need to tell them. You can do this by developing a positioning statement. This is a single sentence that states who you are and why you are different. Some people call this the elevator pitch. Whatever you call it, this statement should be repeated over and over again throughout your digital and other marketing materials. Some people find that their positioning statements tend to ramble on. This is because it can be difficult to sum up all you are in one sentence. However difficult this may be, it is extremely effective. If you're having trouble being concise, remember that a well-worded positioning statement should be easily read aloud in one breath.

- **Separate Yourself From the Competition.** In addition to the positioning statement, you should outline your key marketing messages. What are the five to seven things people *need* to know about you and your business? It is rare for any business to hit everyone in their target demographic list with just one or two key selling points about your business. As the old saying goes "different strokes for different folks." Make sure you can clearly articulate your value and what sets you apart to the various demographics that you are trying to attract. You may even wish to highlight your differentiation in your staff's training exercises. This is where you can address your quality, location, service or some other tangible benefit that your audience *needs* to know about. Listing these points will help you cultivate your overall marketing strategy.

- **Look GREAT.** Digital media demands that businesses look good. Your business deserves to stand out, so make it look GREAT!

Employ a graphic designer to develop a consistent and attractive look across all your digital, interactive and social media spaces. In today's wired society, how your brand looks online is a defining characteristic of the personality communicated by your brand. Everyone from friends to skilled staff members and professional agencies can help you define this personality.

- **Be Interesting.** Infomercials belong on late-night television, not on interactive and social media. Of course, successful commercial messaging is the primary goal of all your efforts, but as you (now) know, constant advertising can be a real turn-off to your audience.

To maintain a level of interest with your audience that will keep them engaged, you must…

- **Give.** Interactive and social media is a two-way line of communication that essentially prohibits you from ramming promotions down your customers' throats. Take the time to educate your community while touting your expertise and passion. It's this passion that inspired you to choose your line of work in the first place, and it's your passion that's going to inspire customers to keep coming back. So tell them about it! Just like in many other mutually enjoyable relationships, it's important that you give before you ask. The same rules still apply on interactive and social media.
- **Publish Consistently.** Much like the aforementioned analogy to a real life relationship, frequency of communication is important. Your brand needs to be seen on a frequent basis in order to keep your name fresh in people's minds.
- **Select the Appropriate Channels.** There are literally hundreds of different interactive and social media channels to choose from. Pick the ones that best support your strategies to reach your target market. For example, a pizza parlor and a plastic surgeon's practice are targeting different people, for different reasons, and will likely choose a very different mix of social media platforms.

- **Promote Thoughtfully.** The core part of any interactive and social media marketing plan is the promotions that you make available to your audience. You should plan out a full year's worth of promotional programs to make sure that your efforts are timely and well received by your audience.
- **Measure Everything.** ANYTHING that receives your time, money or manpower should be measured. The effectiveness of your promotional and non-promotional efforts should be measured in ways that are aimed at moving your business forward. In essence, what are the key aspects that will result in an actual gain in revenue? More calls, appointment requests, online orders? Whatever they are, set your key performance indicators (KPIs) against these things and measure, measure, measure.
- **Monitor. Succeed. Repeat.** Once you've laid out your plan, goals and systems for executing this plan and achieving these goals, you must monitor your progress. Specific members of your core team should collect and report upon the data on a regular basis. When you succeed, see if you can improve upon this success. If you do not, see what you can learn to increase your probability of success in the future!

Interactive and social media marketing are part of the infrastructure upon which consumers make decisions about your business and your competitors. Thoughtful planning and execution will generate a high-powered system that can fuel your business' continued growth and stability for the long haul.

Good luck!!!

APPENDIX I:

∙ ∙

Measuring Your Return On Social Media

As a business owner, your job is to make money. Placing activities that can't be monetized aside, most of your marketing activity should be focused on delivering revenue to your business.

As technology has accelerated, it has become increasingly harder for business owners to keep up with *how* they can measure these marketing results. This is a very understandable issue. Names, platforms and buzzwords change quickly and constantly.

Adding to this confusion is a growing mix of unscrupulous marketing services that are all too eager to bill a company, but are often reluctant to have their progress measured. These vendors tend to hide behind buzzwords and non-revenue generating activities that mask their ignorance when it comes to basic marketing practices and ROI measurement. A great example is the business owner's common fascination with the number of Likes, followers, or +1's. These vanity metrics do *not* deliver financial value, nor true ROI, to the business owner.

The world does not need to be so complicated. We're going to break the return part of a marketing campaign's ROI down to four simple, easy to digest steps that you can use to measure the effectiveness of every marketing dollar spent.

The Four Virtues of a Single Promotional Transaction

1. **Audience**

   For our purposes, the size of your audience is the quantity of people who see your social media promotions. This is usually not equal to the quantity of people who have elected to follow your brand. Rather, this is the quantity of people who actually see your messaging when it goes out.

2. **Value**

   The value of a promotion is the average value of the business that you get from an average customer coming in from that promotion. Note that value is *not* the retail value of the item or service you're promoting. Your promotion is designed to encourage a business transaction, and increase the lifetime value of that customer relationship. The value of this entire transaction is what we'll use for value.

   Say I run a car dealership and I advertise that you can receive a free oil change on the 4th of July. The value of that promotion is definitely not $0, and here is why. At the end of the promotion, to measure the *true* value delivered, we will count the number of transactions, and then add up the total business value of the corresponding purchases from the customers who took advantage of the free oil change. In all likelihood, the service department found other maintenance services and products to sell, and it's even possible that your sales team sold some vehicles to some people who got the free oil change! A couple of vehicle purchases could have raised the average value of the transaction quite a bit. This is an example of how using a loss leader (defined as a promotional transaction with a net negative value to the business in order to drive additional business) like the free oil change can generate significant longer-term business value.

Another important point of this equation about return is to recognize that value is not the overall number corresponding to a transaction size, but instead the *contribution margin* of that transaction.

In other words, your value of a transaction is not the overall transaction, but the amount of that transaction less the cost of goods sold. As an example, if we sold a $20,000 car during our above promotion, we cannot claim a $20,000 value for the transaction. In all likelihood, that car was purchased for $15,000, leaving a $5,000 value to be factored into our average transaction value.

3. **Conversion Rate**
   Conversion rate is the rate at which our audience takes up our promotion.

   Let's continue with our hypothetical car dealer in the above example. If he distributed 1,000 flyers promoting his free oil change, and 100 people showed up to redeem the offer, then his conversion rate was 100/1000, or 10 percent.

4. **Frequency**
   Most digital marketing promotions carry a very small cost for frequency of messaging. As a result, we can put out a large volume of messaging very easily. Frequency is the last important factor in messaging. Remember that different networks demand different frequencies.

APPENDIX II:

● ●

Planning Checklist For Success
Interactive And Social Marketing
For Your Business

Business Name_____

Year/Period_____

- **Choose Success**

  In your own words, write one to two sentences outlining *why* you choose to be successful in interactive and social media marketing:

  _____

  _____

  _____

- **Team Selection**

  List the staff members who will form your interactive marketing team. Be sure to highlight your social captain, who will ultimately be responsible for reporting and monitoring performance:

  _____

  _____

  _____

- **Position Yourself**

  Develop your positioning statement, one sentence that says who you are and why you are different. Make sure it can be read aloud in one breath.

  _____

  _____

  _____

- **Separate Yourself From the Competition**

  What are the five to seven things people _need_ to know about your business?

  _____

  _____

  _____

- **Look GREAT**

  Your digital graphics contain:

  _____

  _____

  _____

- **Give and Be Interesting**

  I will make a commitment to broadcast interesting and educational information on the following topics related to my business. I will do this so I resist the urge to talk about my business, or myself, all the time. These topics will help my audience stay more interested and engaged with my brand, and they will prevent me from looking like a pushy salesperson.

  _____

  _____

  _____

- **Promote Thoughtfully**

  I will keep at least __ percent of my messages non-promotional to better connect with my community. (Hint: At least 80 percent is considered best practice)

- **Select the Appropriate Channels**

  The interactive and social media channels that best support my strategies to reach my target market are:

  _____

  _____

  _____

  _____

- **Measure Everything**

  I will measure the effectiveness of my promotional and non-promotional efforts on interactive and social media with the following quantifiable metrics:

  _____

  _____

  _____

  _____

- **Monitor. Succeed. Repeat**

  The person primarily responsible for collecting performance data is:

  _____

  He/she will provide _____ with the performance data on a _____ basis.

APPENDIX III:

··

Trends

The very nature of technology ensures that any chapter about trends in technology is certain to be obsolete the second it gets spat out of the printing press. In fact, this page is already obsolete because it references the printing press. We can all probably agree that an eBook reference would have been more appropriate.

While we're renegotiating our book deal, let's remember the real point, which is that these trends are constantly changing. Therefore, it's best to visit our blog at www.totalsocialsolutions.com/blog for the most up-to-date information regarding specific trends in technology and interactive and social media marketing.

Social Media Encompasses More Search Functions

People are constantly changing the way they use the internet. In 2010, when Facebook was only a couple years old (but had already virtually destroyed MySpace), search and SEO strategies were focused on a "publish or perish" paradigm. Website owners were rewarded for high volume content production and article marketing with high search rankings.

At this time, social media had very little to do with search, or with a business' digital marketing strategy. Social media was a place that was mostly occupied by individuals – many of whom were playing Farmville and Mafia Wars, as you might recall – in addition to a rare few businesses.

Today, social media and SEO are slowly growing closer together. When your clients search for the next great spa to visit, they are likely to ask their friends on Twitter or seek out reviews for businesses on Yelp. Many consumers find search rankings on Google to be a less reliable indicator than crowd-sourced opinion.

Their reasoning is sound. Again, search platforms like Google have a tendency to reward people who continually produce freshly written content. The truth is that your business can deliver great prices and excellent customer service without your writing a single word. Your customers, on the other hand, are often all too eager to publish their opinions about your services, thereby giving you (and review sites like Yelp) credence.

In addition, the search world has a new player in Facebook. Facebook's Graph Search now lets users enter human language searches such as "spas my friends like" to extract answers from the Facebook network. Social-based search will have a massive impact on the ways in which people select service providers.

As these two mediums converge, we begin to see that success in social media, together with success in SEO, comprise your overall comprehensive digital marketing strategy. The best businesses can – and should – be successful at both.

Online Reputation

Reputation monitoring is an important part of any marketing campaign. Domino's Pizza famously had a pair of rogue employees film themselves performing all sorts of unspeakable, unsanitary acts in one of the Domino's kitchens…with Domino's food. It took Domino's more than two days to publicly respond to this video. By that time, more than one million people had already watched the footage. The damage caused to the company is difficult to measure, but a faster response would have made it easy for news outlets to present a balanced story. This would have mitigated this video's negative impact.

Every business has an online reputation, and monitoring this reputation is a critical part of doing business in today's world. Failing to do so is as careless as failing to count the money in your cash register at the end of the day. Both are foolish oversights on the part of the business manager.

There are many free ways to monitor your online reputation. Spend a little time searching for one that will work for you.

Many paid-for online monitoring solutions offer enhancements, such as:

- Monitoring online review sites that would otherwise go unmonitored
- Automatically judging the tenor of the online conversations about your business
- Proactively suggesting how to combat negative online discussions

Evolution of Social Search

Microsoft launched the Bing search engine with a brilliant marketing tag line, calling it a "decision engine." As a business owner, your marketing efforts are dedicated to changing the decision-making criteria that your customers use. All of the techniques and efforts in this book describe ways to communicate with your community in order to influence their decision-making process.

From the perspective of decision-making, internet usage continues to furiously evolve.

- *Phase I* – traditional ideas, new platform
  The initial push was an extension of traditional brick-and-mortar businesses. The Better Business Bureau, ConsumerReports.com and YellowPages.com were popular sites, allowing people to perform their traditional fact checking much faster.

- *Phase II* – search
  The advent of free, effective search engines changed the way people made decisions. Rather than having to *know* which sites were the authorities on a particular business, internet users could simply type their questions into search engines and browse through the results.

  Savvy business owners quickly realized the power of this decision-making paradigm and took steps to exploit it. The race between search engine providers and business owners continues today. Search engines use unpublished algorithms to rank websites, while business owners spend enormous budgets to try to figure out these algorithms in order to achieve a high ranking. Search engine optimization has influenced our marketing strategies in a bizarre way. It rewards local business owners based on their abilities to publish content and connect to other businesses when, in reality, it ought to issue rewards based upon an objective measure of a business' success.

- *Phase III* – social search
  Consumers continue to be more privy to the workings of the internet. They have learned that a smart business owner with a decent marketing budget can manipulate his search engine results. You can find this out for yourself… do a search for "mesothelioma" and look at the results. The internet abounds with lawyers interested in mesothelioma lawsuits, and through

savvy internet marketing they have pushed down useful educational sites.

As consumers grow more wary of generic search engines, they have begun to turn to other sources when making their decisions about a business. Trusted peer-based reviews are a growing part of the decision-making process today. Companies like Amazon, Yelp, Facebook and Google all incorporate social and peer-based reviews to assist with the search and decision-making processes.

A few important things to remember about social search:

- **Filtering.** Social search sites continue to update their strategies regarding how they filter out spurious, poorly thought-out and unhelpful reviews. How authentic and useful a review is perceived to be is now extremely important.
- **Verifying Identities.** Social search sites are improving the authenticity of their users. Some even require that you use your real name, identifying yourself using real-world paperwork like bills or driver's licenses.
- **Identifying Influential Customers.** Business owners are increasingly interested in understanding how influential an individual customer can be online. Smart business owners acknowledge that all clients are not equal, and that imparting preferential treatment on influential customers can cause a halo effect that brings business in the door.
- **Selecting Quality.** Social search sites are beginning to look for high-quality, filtered reviews. The new challenge for business owners is not to author this high-quality text themselves, but to encourage their customers to write it.

Now that online reviews and the sites where they're featured are seen as trusted, credentialed sources of high-quality recommendations, it's clear that consumers are turning to them more than ever.

APPENDIX IV:

· ·

The Value Of A Phone Call

The million-dollar question when it comes to marketing efforts is: *can you measure your return?*

And we're not just talking about on social and interactive media, but from a bigger-picture business perspective. You can easily figure out your VALUE of a phone call using three simple inputs and the worksheet below:

1. Average Customer Ticket ($)
   When a patient comes in for a treatment, on average, how much do they spend? You should know that number right away or, at the very least, your office manager should. Simply take your gross revenue for a period (i.e. annually), and divide it by the number of *paying* patient encounters for that same period.

2. Gross Margin/Profit (%)
   What is the gross profit, or, average revenue minus average cost of goods sold, for an average procedure in your office? We know it's mostly in the range of 50 percent to 60 percent. That's something your accountant should be able to tell you right off your P&L statement.

3. Call Conversion Rate (%)
    In other words, out of 100 phone calls coming into your practice, how many of those result in a consultation or an appointment?

PHONE CALL VALUATION WORKSHEET

Practice Name: _____

Average Customer Ticket: $_____

Gross Margin/Profit: %_____

Phone Call Conversion Rate: %_____

Value of a Phone Call: $_____

APPENDIX V:

● ●

Trends In Social Media Impacting
Medical Aesthetics

In 2012, you probably didn't think social media could get much hotter. This might be due to the fact that, according to a survey on mayoseitzmediamonitor.com, people spent 33 percent more time on social media in 2012 than they did in 2011. This trend is only going to get hotter with the continued adaptation of mobile and tablet technologies.

With this in mind, it's easy to say that social media is, quite literally, changing the world. Let's look at it from a macro perspective. Foreign dictators are being overthrown with the same social media tools you all have available to you today…yet we have weekly discussions with cosmetic surgeons who say "I can't get a Botox patient to come in using Facebook!"

That's kind of like going on a fishing trip, coming back with an empty pail and blaming the rod. What's to blame is the way in which we're using this tool.

Let's view this on an even larger scale. Our team attended the Consumer Electronics Show (CES) in January 2013 in Las Vegas. We were in a social media forum, and we were surrounded by more than 100 social media professionals. During this forum they asked how many of us were measuring our economic return on social media. A meager 3 percent of the audience raised their hands. This made it clear that people are extremely caught up in value metrics that don't matter.

Social media is about a dialogue that is broadcasted. It's about relationships vs. selling. Community building vs. advertising. This is what you're doing. Social media is like an email list on steroids. It's a community that you're building around your brand.

Don't just take our word for it. The biggest of the big, the people who are making millions of dollars on social media – Lady Gaga, Justin Bieber, Taylor Swift – participate in this world all the time. All day long they're connecting with fans. They're sending out hundreds, maybe even thousands, of posts that have absolutely nothing to do with their latest project or anything they're selling. Instead, they post to connect.

Here's a great example. Taylor Swift recently launched an album through social media. It sold tens of millions of copies. A tremendous success by anyone's standards. Social media gives you the opportunity to be in front of your target on a daily basis where you sit in that trusted friends and family circle on their news feed. But to be successful, you have to do this right.

By the very nature of being in that news feed, you've earned their trust. Now you have to make sure that your presence is well managed if you plan to stay there. A well-managed social media community drives the lifetime value of patient relationships through brand stickiness. This is where you win on social media. This is when patients don't even pay attention to that Botox® deal on LivingSocial or Groupon from some other doctor down the street because they have loyalty to you; because your business is now within this friends and family nodule. You've now got them in a place where they feel more affinity and allegiance to your brand.

APPENDIX VI:

Additional Reading

There exists a huge volume of material that discusses, analyzes, and recommends marketing and promotions strategies.

Some we recommend include:

- *Influence* by Robert Cialdini
- *The Tipping Point* by Malcolm Gladwell
- *SPIN Selling* by Neil Rackham
- *Nudge: Improving Decisions About Health, Wealth, and Happiness* by Richard H. Thaler and Cass R. Sunstein

www.ingramcontent.com/pod-product-compliance
Lightning Source LLC
Chambersburg PA
CBHW072036190526
45165CB00017B/945